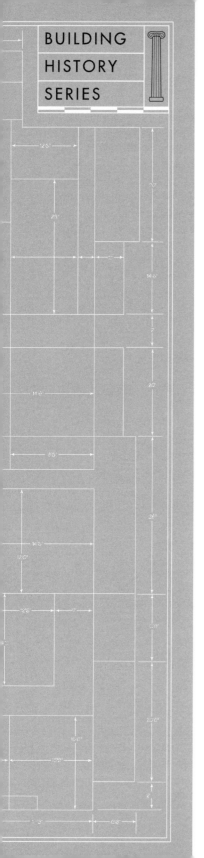

BUILDING
HISTORY
SERIES

# THE
# PANAMA
# CANAL

by Tim McNeese

Lucent Books, Inc., San Diego, California

Library of Congress Cataloging-in-Publication Data

McNeese, Tim.
    The Panama Canal / by Tim McNeese.
        p.    cm. — (Building history series)
    Includes bibliographical references and index.
    Summary: Describes the planning and building of the
Panama Canal.
    ISBN 1-56006-425-0 (alk paper)
    1. Panama Canal (Panama)—History—Juvenile literature.
[1. Panama Canal (Panama)—History.]   I. Title.   II. Series.
F1569.C2M34    1997
386'.44'09—dc21                                      96-45623
                                                        CIP
                                                        AC

# Contents

T 23378

# FOREWORD

Throughout history, as civilizations have evolved and prospered, each has produced unique buildings and architectural styles. Combining the need for both utility and artistic expression, a society's buildings, particularly its large-scale public structures, often reflect the individual character traits that distinguish it from other societies. In a very real sense, then, buildings express a society's values and unique characteristics in tangible form. As scholar Anita Abromovitz comments in her book *People and Spaces*, "Our ways of living and thinking—our habits, needs, fear of enemies, aspirations, materialistic concerns, and religious beliefs—have influenced the kinds of spaces that we build and that later surround and include us."

That specific types and styles of structures constitute an outward expression of the spirit of an individual people or era can be seen in the diverse ways that various societies have built palaces, fortresses, tombs, churches, government buildings, sports arenas, public works, and other such monuments. The ancient Greeks, for instance, were a supremely rational people who originated Western philosophy and science, including the atomic theory and the realization that the earth is a sphere. Their public buildings, epitomized by Athens's magnificent Parthenon temple, were equally rational, emphasizing order, harmony, reason, and above all, restraint.

By contrast, the Romans, who conquered and absorbed the Greek lands, were a highly practical people preoccupied with acquiring and wielding power over others. The Romans greatly admired and readily copied elements of Greek architecture, but modified and adapted them to their own needs. "Roman genius was called into action by the enormous practical needs of a world empire," wrote historian Edith Hamilton. "Rome met them magnificently. Buildings tremendous, indomitable, amphitheaters where eighty thousand could watch a spectacle, baths where three thousand could bathe at the same time."

In medieval Europe, God heavily influenced and motivated the people, and religion permeated all aspects of society, molding people's worldviews and guiding their everyday actions. That spiritual mindset is reflected in the most important medieval structure—the Gothic cathedral—which, in a sense, was a model of heavenly cities. As scholar Anne Fremantle so elegantly phrases it, the cathedrals were "harmonious elevations of stone and glass reaching up to heaven to seek and receive the light [of God]."

Our more secular modern age, in contrast, is driven by the realities of a global economy, advanced technology, and mass communications. Responding to the needs of international trade and the growth of cities housing millions of people, today's builders construct engineering marvels, among them towering skyscrapers of steel and glass, mammoth marine canals, and huge and elaborate rapid transit systems, all of which would have left their ancestors, even the Romans, awestruck.

In examining some of humanity's greatest edifices, Lucent Books' Building History Series recognizes this close relationship between a society's historical character and its buildings. Each volume in the series begins with a historical sketch of the people who erected the edifice, exploring their major achievements as well as the beliefs, customs, and societal needs that dictated the variety, functions, and styles of their buildings. A detailed explanation of how the selected structure was conceived, designed, and built, to the extent that this information is known, makes up the majority of the volume.

Each volume in the Lucent Building History Series also includes several special features that are useful tools for additional research. A chronology of important dates gives students an overview, at a glance, of the evolution and use of the structure described. Sidebars create a broader context by adding further details on some of the architects, engineers, and construction tools, materials, and methods that made each structure a reality, as well as the social, political, and/or religious leaders and movements that inspired its creation. Useful maps help the reader locate the nations, cities, streets, and individual structures mentioned in the text; and numerous diagrams and pictures illustrate tools and devices that bring to life various stages of construction. Finally, each volume contains two bibliographies, one for student research, the other listing works the author consulted in compiling the book.

Taken as a whole, these volumes, covering diverse ancient and modern structures, constitute not only a valuable research tool, but also a tribute to the human spirit, a fascinating exploration of the dreams, skills, ingenuity, and dogged determination of the great peoples who shaped history.

# IMPORTANT DATES IN THE BUILDING OF THE PANAMA CANAL

**1882**
Serious excavation work begins on the construction of a sea-level French canal on January 20.

**1825**
The French government begins sending engineers to Panama to consider the best possible canal routes across the isthmus.

*A ship passes through Gatun Locks.*

| 1820 | 1840 | 1860 | 1880 | 1900 |
|------|------|------|------|------|

**1850**
The Clayton-Bulwer Treaty, signed by the United States and Great Britain, guarantees that both nations will share in the building of the Panama Canal.

**1889**
The French Panama Canal Company ceases construction; the United States begins organizing an American canal-building effort.

*A tower of steel and concrete rises during the building of the canal.*

**1903**
Panama, with the aid of the United States, gains its independence from Colombia.

**1908**
December 12—Worst single dynamite accident to occur while constructing the canal; 22 tons of dynamite explode, killing 23 workers and injuring nearly 40 more; cause of explosion was never discovered.

**1913**
Work is completed on the Miraflores Locks; the Culebra Cut, the portion of the canal carved through the Culebra Mountains; and the Gatun Locks; all dry excavation on the Panama Canal ceases; the tugboat *Gatun* is the first to be sent through the locks.

| 1903 | 1906 | 1909 | 1912 | 1915 |

*Theodore Roosevelt*

**1914**
January 7—A crane boat, the *Alexandre La Valley*, makes the first complete passage through the Panama Canal, from the Atlantic to the Pacific side.

August 15—The Panama Canal officially opens.

**1904**
U.S. Senate authorizes payment to Panama for the creation of a ten-mile-wide Canal Zone; the United States begins construction of the canal.

# Introduction

On the afternoon of October 10, 1913, Woodrow Wilson, the president of the United States, pressed a button that set off a huge explosion in a massive earthen dike in the mountains of the small Central American country of Panama. The explosion punched a hole in the dike a hundred feet wide. The waters of Gatun Lake burst through the gap, pouring into the largest ditch humans have ever dug—the Panama Canal.

Slowly the swirling waters of Gatun Lake began to fill the empty trench. For the hundreds of canal workers and engineers watching from the mouth of the Great Cut, this tidal wave of lake water was the completion of a dream.

For hundreds of years before the Panama Canal was completed, people had dreamed of a great waterway connecting

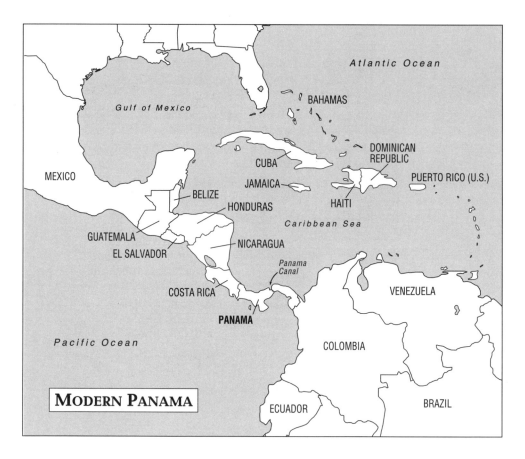

MODERN PANAMA

## PANAMA AND THE NAME GAME

The word *panama* comes from a Cueva Indian word meaning "fisherman" or "plenty of fish." But the land itself has gone by several names. Little is known about the Panamanian isthmus before the arrival of Europeans in the 1500s. Before European colonization, the Indian population of the area numbered between a half million and two million. The region came under Spanish control during the early 1500s. Spain divided its American colonies into bureaucratic regions called viceroyalties. In 1542 Panama became part of the viceroyalty of Peru. Two hundred years later, in 1740, Panama was transferred to the viceroyalty of New Granada. A century later Panama experienced a revolution that caused its separation from Spain. With their new independence, proclaimed on November 28, 1821, the people of Panama joined the freed peoples of the former viceroyalty of New Granada and formed a new nation known as Greater Colombia. This large nation-state included most of modern Venezuela, Ecuador, Colombia, and Panama.

In 1830 Venezuela and Ecuador withdrew from Greater Colombia. Greater Colombia then reorganized and was renamed the Republic of New Granada. Panama then became a department of the Republic of New Granada. When a new constitution was written and adopted in 1863, the Republic of New Granada changed its name back to Colombia. Panama finally declared its independence from Colombia in 1903 with the aid of the United States. Since then, the isthmian region has been known as the Republic of Panama.

the Atlantic and Pacific Oceans. Such a water route would shorten the trip from one ocean to another by eliminating the need to sail eight thousand miles around the entire continent of South America. One obvious location for such a waterway was what is today called the Isthmus of Panama. An isthmus is a narrow strip of land connecting two larger land areas. The Isthmus of Panama varies in width from 130 miles to 30 miles, the shortest distance between the oceans in Central America. This fact made Panama inviting to anyone interested in building a canal in the Western Hemisphere.

*Explorer Vasco Núñez de Balboa claims the Pacific Ocean and the Panamanian isthmus for his benefactor, King Ferdinand of Spain.*

Perhaps the first European to search for a water route connecting the eastern and western shores of the New World was the great Italian explorer Christopher Columbus. In 1498, six years after his first famous voyage to the Americas, Columbus made his third trip there. When he landed on the shores of South America, the inhabitants told him about "a narrow land between two seas." This interested Columbus, since he was looking for a way to continue west in search of Asia. But at that time Columbus could not leave his ships to search for it.

Four years passed before Columbus returned to the New World. Again he heard stories about the "narrow land." It was on this voyage that Columbus found the Isthmus of Panama—the strip of land described in the stories. He found it by traveling up the Chagres River, which cut deeply into the Panamanian interior. His canoe actually came within twelve miles of the Pacific coast. But the mountains halted his inland search.

## BALBOA CROSSES THE ISTHMUS

Ten years passed before a European explorer crossed the mountains that had stopped Columbus. In 1513 a Spanish military leader, or conquistador, named Vasco Núñez de Balboa led a group of soldiers and natives across the isthmus. Hacking their way through the thick jungles, they took nearly a month to reach the top of the Culebra Range, mountains that rise about a thousand feet above sea level.

Off to the south Balboa could see the Pacific Ocean, which he called the Great South Sea. Climbing down the western slope of the mountains, Balboa reached the Pacific four days later. Standing in the tidal waters, Balboa claimed the isthmus for the king of Spain, Ferdinand the Catholic.

Others followed Balboa's journey to the Pacific. His explorations and those a few years later of Pedro Arias de Ávila proved that there was no water route through the isthmus connecting the two vast oceans. However, the narrowness of the isthmus made it a good place to consider building a canal in the future.

## THE FIRST PROPOSAL

In 1529 a Spaniard named Alvaro de Saavedra Ceron made the first known proposal to dig a canal across the isthmus. The canal route he suggested would have begun at Colón, a good, natural harbor on the Atlantic side of Panama, and would have followed the Chagres River.

Saavedra's ideas reached the Spanish king, Charles V. Charles favored building a canal across the isthmus for several reasons. Sailing around the southern tip of South America was dangerous. Later called the Strait of Magellan, these coastal waters were rocky, and the strait was narrow and subject to frequent storms. Also, the Spanish could avoid contact with the Portuguese, who were colonizing to the south. Charles ordered his advisors and engineering experts to come up with a plan for a canal. But those who studied the geography of the isthmus

*Panama's proximity to the Pacific Ocean made it a bustling port. Explorers and merchants from around the world set sail for the isthmus.*

told him such a water route could not be built. A later Spanish king, Philip II, also had an interest in a canal through the isthmus. His advisors, too, decided that a canal was impossible, quoting from the Bible the warning: "What God has joined together, let no man put asunder." The Spanish king felt certain that the mountain range through the isthmus would always stand in the way of any attempted canal. To ensure that no one would prove him wrong, Philip issued a royal order that anyone who tried to build such a canal would be put to death. This official decree kept God-fearing Spanish monarchs from considering a canal across the isthmus for more than two hundred years!

## THE DREAM IS REVIVED

Not until the early nineteenth century would people again make plans for a canal in Central America. In 1811 Baron Alexander von Humboldt, a German-born naturalist, published a paper suggesting nine possible canal routes through the

## THE SHAPE OF A NATION

The Isthmus of Panama is a long, narrow strip of land that extends about 480 miles from Costa Rica to the north to the South American nation of Colombia to the south. The distance across the isthmus varies from 130 miles at its widest point to only 30 miles at its narrowest. On a map, the country looks much like the letter S lying on its side. Panama is about the size of the state of South Carolina, covering about 30,000 square miles. Because of its narrowness, the Panamanian isthmus was considered for centuries to be the best place for a canal, since less excavation would be required due to the short length of such a canal.

For approximately seventy-five years the area in Panama where the canal was finally built was known as the Panama Canal Zone. This was a strip of land that cut across the Republic of Panama. The canal runs through this former zone, which was established by treaty in 1903 between the United States and Panama. The United States paid Panama each year for use of the zone. By 1955 the annual payment had been raised to nearly two million dollars. The zone covered 553 square miles, or a strip approximately 10 miles wide and 40 miles long. About 40 percent of that area is underwater today. In 1977 the United States agreed to a new canal treaty with Panama that turned the Canal Zone over to the Panamanians in 1979.

Americas. Humboldt wrote that a canal through Nicaragua would be the easiest to build. However, he had few facts to support his opinion. Humboldt drew his proposed routes from inaccurate maps and old books. He had visited South America, exploring the Amazon River and climbing the Andes mountains. But he never visited either Nicaragua or Panama.

But no matter; his proposals were taken seriously. No longer was the Spanish government blind to the possibilities of creating such a water route, as King Philip II had been. Within ten years of Humboldt's proposal, Spain set up a company to explore building a canal at one of the nine suggested locations. But Spain moved too slowly. By 1825 Spain had lost its New World colonies, except Cuba and Puerto Rico, and at the same time lost interest in building a canal. Although Spain's dominance in the New World had ended, worldwide support for a transportation route across the isthmus grew.

*In 1811, Baron Alexander von Humboldt, a distinguished naturalist, revived the dream of building a canal in Central America.*

## Plans Begin to Take Shape

Several European nations, including France, England, and Germany, had an interest in building a canal. The United States also began considering such a project. But the French led the way. For twenty years, beginning in 1825, the French government sent several groups of engineers to the isthmus. The French engineers explored Humboldt's proposed canal sites.

The French government decided that a railroad would be cheaper to build than a canal and would make building a water route easier and cheaper to construct in the future. In 1838 the Republic of New Granada, today the nations of Colombia and Panama, gave the French government permission to build a railroad through the isthmus. Meanwhile, preparations for a canal continued. The work progressed slowly, however, since no French company was willing to risk millions of dollars on either a railroad or a canal.

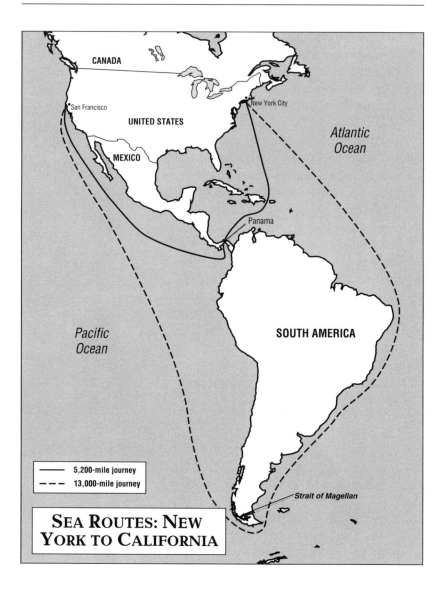

CANADA

San Francisco

New York City

UNITED STATES

*Atlantic
Ocean*

MEXICO

Panama

*Pacific
Ocean*

SOUTH AMERICA

——— 5,200-mile journey
– – – 13,000-mile journey

Strait of Magellan

**SEA ROUTES: NEW
YORK TO CALIFORNIA**

## AMERICA BECOMES INVOLVED

While the French dawdled, the Americans took the lead. In January 1848 a sawmill worker on the American River in northern California found gold nuggets in the mill's water runoff and word of the find soon spread. People immediately flocked to California, most of them Americans from the eastern United States. Many took passage on oceangoing ships, sailing from New York City, around the South American continent, to

San Francisco, California. The voyage was thirteen thousand miles long and took five months to complete.

This lengthy journey prompted the opening of an overland route through Panama. A traveler could take passage on a steamship from the eastern seaboard to the Panamanian coast. Passengers then had to paddle up the Chagres River by canoe, then trek by mule and on foot through the jungles and over the mountains of the steamy isthmus. The threat of death was everywhere. Unsanitary drinking water, rotten food, poisonous jungle snakes, and disease-carrying mosquitoes worried even the hardiest travelers. After completing the journey, a traveler from Massachusetts wrote: "I have no time to give reasons but . . . in fear of God and the love of man, to one and all, for no consideration come this route. I have nothing to say for the other routes but do not take this one."

With thousands of people passing through the isthmus, Americans revived the idea of a railroad. The Panama Railroad Company was created in the spring of 1849. By January 1855 it had built a railroad across the isthmus. The railroad cut the

*Crowds gather in Culebra, Panama—the terminus of the American-built railroad. A one-way trip across the isthmus cost travelers twenty-five dollars in gold but saved them nearly two weeks in travel time.*

time it took to travel across the isthmus from nearly two weeks to just over three hours. A one-way ticket cost travelers twenty-five dollars in gold.

## ENGLAND FLEXES ITS MUSCLES

All the building activity and traffic on the isthmus increased interest in a ship canal. In line with Humboldt's suggestions over forty years earlier, Great Britain and the United States both favored a canal in Nicaragua, about three hundred miles north of the American-built railroad. But some British leaders did not want America to build a canal in Central America. Determined to keep the Americans out of Nicaragua, Great Britain took action. On New Year's Day 1849 a British gunboat dropped anchor off the Nicaraguan coast of San Juan del Norte and seized the American settlement there.

Rather than fight, the United States and Great Britain worked out an agreement. The result was the Clayton-Bulwer Treaty of 1850. This treaty guaranteed that if a canal was ever attempted in Central America, it would be a project shared by both nations. In the event of war the Canal Zone would remain neutral and open to shipping. In exchange for this agreement by the United States, Britain promised not to interfere with the building of the American railroad through Panama.

Fifty years had passed since Humboldt's Central American explorations and his nine proposals for an isthmian canal. Engineers and surveyors had come and gone. Treaties and other international agreements had been made. Various nations' interest in a canal had grown, some nearly to the point of military conflict. A railroad *had* been built connecting the Atlantic and Pacific coasts, but the dream of a canal remained ever distant. A generation would pass before construction on an isthmian canal began. That project was taken up, not by the United States or Great Britain, but by France.

# The French Attempt a Canal

# 1

The American-built railroad and the treaty between Great Britain and the United States inspired France to act. If France was to play a key role in the Western Hemisphere—as it wished to do—a French canal could prove crucial to attaining that goal.

The French already had experience with canal building. Between 1859 and 1869 they directed construction of the Suez Canal, a hundred-mile-long canal linking the Mediterranean Sea with the Gulf of Suez. Building this sea-level canal gave France a new national confidence and placed it in the position of being the world's foremost canal builder.

## Lesseps and France Lead the Way

The man who had overseen the building of the Suez Canal for France was Ferdinand de Lesseps. With the Suez project behind him, Lesseps believed he was the logical choice for heading a Panama canal construction project. By 1875 an organization called the French Committee for Cutting the Interoceanic Canal was founded, and Lesseps was chosen as its president.

In 1876 the committee sent one of its engineers to Central America to study possible canal routes. His name was Lucien Napoléon-Bonaparte Wyse, a French naval lieutenant and descendent of the French emperor and general Napoléon I. After tromping through the Panamanian jungle for months, Wyse returned to France and reported to the committee. He told them that a canal could be built over Panama's Culebra Range. This would require a series of locks, which are watertight compartments that raise and lower ships to different levels. The locks were needed, said Wyse, since the Atlantic and Pacific tides and sea levels are different from each other. (Sea levels are not the same in all parts of the world, and they change constantly with rising and lowering tides. At times, the sea levels on Panama's Atlantic and Pacific coasts differ by as much as twenty feet.)

Lesseps refused to listen to Wyse. The old Frenchman had built a sea-level canal in the Suez and saw no reason why such a canal could not work in Panama. Lesseps sent Wyse back to Panama, telling him in no uncertain terms what he wanted to hear when Wyse returned: "If you come back with a favorable report on a sea-level canal on that route [along the Panama Railroad line] I shall favor it."

Wyse had no idea how a sea-level canal could be built on the Panamanian isthmus. He knew only that it would require carving a nine-mile-long tunnel through the Panamanian mountains, which seemed impossible. Nevertheless, Wyse went ahead with plans for a sea-level canal. He selected a route following the American-built Panamanian rail line, just as Lesseps wished.

He negotiated an agreement with the Colombians that gave the French permission to build a canal in Panama.

*When the French decided to build a canal in Central America, acclaimed engineer Ferdinand de Lesseps accepted command of the project.*

He also traveled to New York to arrange the purchase of the railroad after he learned that its American owner controlled the right-of-way necessary for the canal construction.

## AN ALTERNATE CANAL PLAN

When Wyse returned to France, an excited Lesseps called for a meeting of those interested in a canal in Panama. During the first session of the International Congress for Consideration of an Interoceanic Canal, Lesseps argued for a sea-level canal. Although Lesseps was not a trained engineer, his success with the Suez Canal won him many supporters when it came time to decide what type of canal to build.

But not everyone agreed with Lesseps. A fellow Frenchman, Adolphe Godin de Lepinay, the chief engineer with the French Department of Bridges and Highways, argued that no machin-

ery existed that could cut a sea-level canal through the Panamanian mountain range. To build such a canal, workers would
have to dig to a minimum depth of 29½ feet. The bottom of the
canal would be 72 feet wide. These measurements were approximately the same as that of the Suez Canal. It was estimated that
workers would have to remove 157 million cubic yards of dirt for
the canal. An eight- or nine-mile cut measuring 300 feet deep
would have to be made through the Culebra Range. Just to cut
through the Culebra alone would require workers and machines
to remove 150 million cubic yards of earth.

Lepinay felt that Lesseps's work with a sea-level canal in the
Suez did not qualify him to influence French plans in Panama.
Lepinay felt the two projects had little in common, with the land,
sea, and climates differing widely. In one speech Lepinay said:

At Suez there is a lack of water, the terrain is easy, the
land nearly the same level as the sea; in spite of the

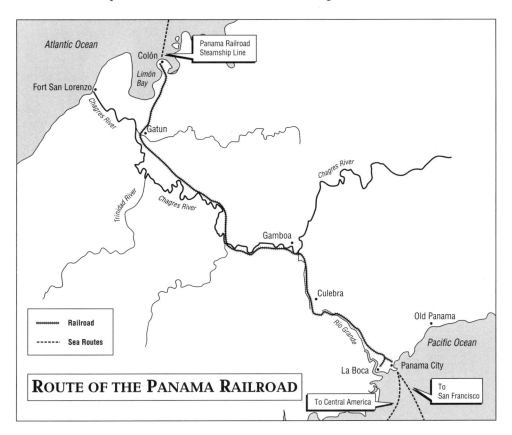

ROUTE OF THE PANAMA RAILROAD

heat, it is a perfectly healthy climate. In tropical America, there is too much water, the terrain is mostly rock, the land has considerable relief [elevations], and finally the country is literally poisoned.

Lepinay believed that Lesseps was headed in an altogether wrong direction. He proposed damming two Panamanian rivers: the Chagres on the Atlantic coast and the Rio Grande on the Pacific side. Damming the rivers would create two great lakes on both sides of the Culebra Range. Locks could then be built to raise the water level of these inland lakes to lift ships over the mountain and down to the oceans below.

But Lesseps would not listen—not even to his son, Charles, who was a trained and talented engineer. Charles did not share his father's enthusiasm for a sea-level canal in Panama. He considered the plan a very big gamble. Charles even said on one occasion to his famous, yet stubborn, father:

> What do you wish to find at Panama? Money? You will not bother about money at Panama any more than you

## WHAT IS A CANAL?

Simply put, canals are waterways built by humans. Generally a canal will connect natural bodies of water such as rivers, lakes, and oceans. Most canals are built to carry either people or goods from one place to another by a shorter route. Some canals provide irrigation for farmland. Other canals carry water to cities from faraway lakes and reservoirs. Still others carry off sewage or are built to drain swamps.

Some countries, such as Russia, China, and the Netherlands, have many canals. China boasts the longest canal in the world, the thousand-mile-long Grand Canal of China. The city of Venice, Italy, is built around canals. Instead of streets, Venetian people and their visitors get around on canals.

Canals are always level and flat. If they are built below the level of the waterways they connect, they usually have only one level. This type of canal is sometimes called a sea-level canal. Other canals must be built at several different levels. These canals are constructed in sections,

did at Suez. Glory? You've had enough glory. Why not leave that to someone else? All of us who have worked at your side are entitled to a rest. Certainly the Panama project is grandiose, and I believe that it can be carried through, but consider the risks those who direct it will run! You succeeded at Suez by a miracle. Should not one be satisfied with accomplishing one miracle in a lifetime and not hope for a second? If you decide to proceed with this, if nothing will stop you . . . if you want me to assist you, then I will take whatever comes. I shall not complain no matter what happens. All that I am I owe to you; what you have given me, you have the right to take away.

When faced with his son's cautionary words, Lesseps simply told Charles that his mind was made up.

## RAISING THE MONEY FOR A CANAL

Lesseps pushed ahead with his plans for the sea-level canal. At his urging, the canal committee formed the Panama Canal

usually called locks. Locks carry boats and ships uphill and downhill.

A lock can be described as a large watertight compartment or box, built big enough to hold an entire boat. Each lock has gates on both ends. The gate connected to the lower section of a canal may open and allow a boat to enter. Then the gate is shut behind it. Water is pumped into the lock, which fills up, causing the boat to rise, much like a toy boat floating in a filling bathtub. The boat is raised in the lock until the level of the water in the lock is the same as the level of water in the next lock. Then the doors of the next lock open, and the boat enters the second lock. Once a boat travels through a series of locks, it will finally reach the level of the body of water ahead of it.

Locks, then, may carry a boat or ship uphill or downhill. For a lock to help a boat travel downhill, the lock is drained, allowing the boat to drop to the water level in the next lock down. This process is followed until the boat has successfully been taken through the locks of the canal.

Company to oversee the financing and construction of a canal. Lesseps was elected its president. One of the company's many duties was fund-raising. The canal was expected to cost about one billion francs. Company officials hoped to raise four hundred million francs (about eighty million dollars) in their first fund drive, held on August 6 and 7, 1879. But the drive raised a disappointing thirty million francs.

In fact, the French drives to raise money for the Panama canal almost always came up short. Despite Lesseps's enthusiasm for the project, the French public remained uninterested. Also, some of those in a position to influence public opinion—newspaper publishers and politicians—offered their support, but only in return for payment. Lesseps so badly wanted public opinion on his side that on occasion he did try to buy the support of influential French citizens.

Lesseps also tried to boost enthusiasm and raise money for the canal by going on a speaking tour across France. He raised about six hundred million francs, which fell short of his goal. So Lesseps also campaigned for money in other European countries, including England, the Netherlands, and Belgium. Early in 1880 Lesseps even made a fund-raising tour of the United States. Although he received a polite reception, few Americans with money to contribute had an interest in supporting a French canal.

## PROBLEMS BUILDING THE CANAL

Raising money was only one of the many difficulties the French had in building a canal in Panama. The first teams of engineers and workers sent to Panama found many problems waiting for them in the jungles of the isthmus, including poisonous snakes, deadly cats such as pumas and jaguars, and insects and parasites, including mosquitoes, spiders, flies, ticks, and chiggers. Mosquitoes thrived in the humid, swampy jungles, spreading malaria and yellow fever.

Panama's wet climate caused other problems, too. Iron and steel rusted in a matter of days. Workers' shoes grew mold overnight. At the end of each working day, the men found their clothes drenched from rain and sweat. The next morning the workers put those same soaked and foul-smelling clothes back on.

More troubles surfaced in September 1882, when an earthquake struck Panama. It lasted less than a minute but did

*In Tavernilla, Panama, a French excavator removes dirt and debris from the canal site. Canal work in Panama was complicated by the wet, hot climate, which caused machines to rust and workers to become soaked with rain and sweat.*

much damage. The rail line was hardest hit. In some places the rail bed sank eight to ten feet, twisting the track out of shape. Back in France such catastrophes alarmed many investors. But Lesseps was always on hand to calm everyone. To put off fears of other destructive tremors, he simply *promised* there would be no more earthquakes.

Nature struck in other ways. The Chagres River, which coursed deeply into Panama, flooded often when heavy rains came to the isthmus, causing mud slides. Such disasters caused delays in the progress of the digging along the canal route.

The problems in Panama did not stop people from signing on to work on the canal. By December 1881 two thousand men were on the canal site. Few of the workers were Panamanians, as the native population showed little interest in work on the canal. Some came from other Latin American countries, including Venezuela and Colombia. The majority, however, were English-speaking blacks from the Caribbean island nation of Jamaica. In fact, most of those working for the French canal effort were black, including about five hundred black Americans

## THOSE DEADLY MOSQUITOES

Canal workers in Panama faced many hardships—among them strenuous work, oppressive heat, inferior food, and constant boredom. But risk of disease outweighed all the others, with often deadly results. The diseases of malaria and yellow fever killed thousands of workers all along the isthmus.

*A yellow fever patient reposes in an isolation cage to prevent the spread of the deadly disease. Thousands of canal workers died from malaria and yellow fever during the course of the construction.*

from several southern states and the city of New Orleans. Many white Americans were present also. They worked as engineers, technicians, mechanics, and contractors.

Barracks for housing the workers were built on concrete pillars to keep out floodwater and rats. Each building was big enough for fifty bunks. The barracks had long porches, called verandas, running along all four sides. Engineers lived in cottages built along the eastern shore. Each cottage was one story, painted white with green shutters, and featured lots of windows.

The French would be long gone from the canal before anyone identified mosquitoes as the carriers of these dreaded diseases. The word *malaria* comes from an Italian phrase *mala aria*, which means "bad air." Many blamed bad air, or poisonous swamp gas, as the source of malaria. In fact, each disease was carried by different types of mosquitoes.

Both diseases are common to tropical regions such as Panama. The symptoms of a typical attack of malaria included chills, followed by high fever and a constant thirst. When the fever broke, the patient broke out in a heavy sweat. Even those who survived the symptoms developed acute depression later. Also, the disease could return. To fight malaria, canal workers took doses of quinine, a bitter-tasting white powder made from the bark of the cinchona tree.

There was no medicine to combat yellow fever, however. The symptoms were much like those of malaria but also included painful headaches and severe pain in the leg and back muscles. After a day or so the patient began to turn yellow, especially around the face and eyes. The disease's terminal stages included throwing up great amounts of dark blood, often called black vomit. Then the body temperature dropped, and the patient became very cold. Once a patient reached that stage, death came in a matter of hours.

Experts estimate that at least twenty thousand workers died during the years of the French canal project from the effects of these two frightening, and misunderstood, tropical diseases.

The men found some basic comforts in these houses. Many of the laborers were not happy with their work, however, and only about ten out of every hundred workers stayed on the job in Panama after six months. In addition, when each day's work ended, the men usually found themselves bored. There were no cafes or restaurants, no libraries, no theaters, no concerts. Reading by even the dimmest light attracted hundreds of insects.

The work was difficult. In the uplands, away from the coasts, much of the work was done by steam shovel and by hand, with picks and shovels and wheelbarrows. Each worker was paid according to the amount of earth he moved in a wheelbarrow. Most workers were paid well for the times: about a dollar to a dollar and a half a day. But the work was back-breaking. Despite the difficult work, progress was made on the canal's construction. By September 1883 the canal was host to at least ten thousand men. By the year's end thirteen thousand could be found toiling on the canal project. By May 1883 nearly nineteen thousand people were at work on the isthmian canal.

Work on the canal—what the French were already calling La Grande Tranchée, meaning The Great Trench—had begun on January 20, 1882. Dynamite charges were ignited to blast

away rock or loosen soil for excavation. The steam shovels followed, scooping up the earth in great loads. Much hand labor was required for the finish work as men, armed with picks and shovels, went down into the trench to level out the digging.

*(Below) To house the great number of canal workers, laborers constructed large, fifty-bunk barracks. (Left) The more fortunate engineers lived in small, one-story cottages.*

*Laborers wield picks and shovels while working in the base of Panama's great trench. Although the French relied on powerful steam shovels to excavate the bulk of earth from the trench, exhausting manual labor was needed to level out the dirt.*

## EQUIPMENT AND OBSTACLES

The French had brought together some of the best digging and hauling equipment in the world for their canal construction. Along the canal route one could find more than thirty steam shovels, fifty railroad locomotives, and over three thousand railroad flatcars and dirt trucks. The trains and trucks hauled the earth and rock from the digging site and disposed of the refuse, using much of it to fill in lowlands and swamps. In addition there were hundreds of tugboats, dredges, water pumps, rock drills, and thousands of hand tools.

But all the equipment in the world could not save the French canal project in Panama from failing. Despite their progress on the canal, the immense obstacle of the Culebra Range always lay ahead. The French began, but would never finish, the cut through the mountain. For all the problems workers and engineers faced on the canal site, bigger problems were brewing back in France.

## THE SLAVEN DREDGE

A new and massive piece of machinery was put to work on the canal: the Slaven dredge. Built in Philadelphia, Pennsylvania, and towed by ship to Panama, the dredge measured 120 feet long by 30 feet wide.

The machine looked something like a giant escalator, and it did two important jobs. It removed earth and rock from the canal, and it deposited them away from the work site. Several steam engines powered each dredge, turning large wheels that ran an endless line of iron scoops, or buckets. Each bucket held about one cubic meter of earth and ran up out of the excavation to the top of a wooden tower. Once there—between 50 and 70 feet high—water blasted the dirt and gravel through great pipes, or chutes, measuring 4 feet across. These pipes deposited the earth and rock at least 180 feet back from the trench where the men were working.

The Slaven dredge worked wonders. Most of these immense machines ran around the clock. They made great progress down on the flats of the Atlantic end of the canal project, where a steam shovel might sink in the mud.

*A massive French dredge scoops up mud and rocks in the Pacific channel.*

The Panama Canal Company was slowly going broke. Lesseps found himself having to cope with charges of theft and fraud, bribery and waste. Funds were running low, because huge sums had been paid to corrupt politicians and newspaper editors. Work crews began to lose hope of ever finishing the canal.

Lesseps managed to keep the project going several more years until the summer of 1887. By then hundreds of millions of francs had been spent, and the end of the work on the canal was nowhere in site. Everyone in Panama had known for years that a sea-level canal was going to be impossible. In January 1887 Lesseps's own Canal Advisory Commission shifted its support to construction of a lock canal. But Lesseps stubbornly would not listen. Only when the French government refused to authorize a national lottery to raise badly needed funds for the canal project did Lesseps finally surrender his dream of a sea-level canal.

## ABANDONING THE DREAM

His decision to switch from a sea-level to a lock canal came too late. Such a change would require at least another five hundred million francs, and company funds were nearly gone. Lesseps pushed for passage of a national lottery to raise more money for the canal. But even when the French Chamber of Deputies, the national legislative body, passed the lottery bill, few French citizens supported it. Nothing was left for Lesseps but bankruptcy and personal disgrace. On December 15, 1888, the French chamber voted down his request to form a new canal company to replace the old one.

When a newspaper reporter went to Lesseps's home and told him the news of the Chamber of Deputies decision, the old Frenchman wept bitterly, holding a handkerchief over his face to muffle the noise of his sobs. He cried aloud:

> This is impossible! This is horrible! I did not believe the French Chamber would sacrifice the interests of the nation. They forget the milliard and a half [billion and a half francs] of the savings of the French people that are compromised by this vote, and they could have saved all this by a firm decision. This will be a triumph for our enemies, and a disaster to our flag.

The decision spelled the end of the French canal construction project in Panama. On February 4, 1889, the French

*Dredges fell into disrepair after being abandoned by the French. Lesseps's lofty dreams of a sea-level canal came to a sad end on May 15, 1889.*

Panama Canal Company halted all new projects. Work in Panama continued off and on for a few months. But on May 15 the steam dredges and huge power shovels were silenced. All work stopped. The workers left their jobs and the isthmus behind. They also left their equipment just where it was when the work ended. Rust soon covered the machinery, followed by the jungle, as vines and undergrowth soon hid dredges, steam shovels, and locomotives. The workers' villages were abandoned, becoming gloomy ghost towns.

The canal, as Lesseps envisioned it, had proven impossible to accomplish. The French had spent years digging a trench through the Culebra Range. When the work at Culebra was abandoned, the cut was far from complete. The mountains had beaten the French. The French dream of a Panamanian canal was lost forever.

# 2

# THE UNITED STATES PLANS A CANAL

In 1889, when Lesseps's company went broke, the French stopped work on the Panama Canal. But the company kept a small number of employees in the canal area for another ten years, hoping to keep open possibilities to begin work again in the future. In the meantime the French were looking for some-one to buy them out, take over the project, and help them cut their losses. Finally their opportunity came in 1898 with the outbreak of war.

## AMERICA SEES THE NEED

The United States and Spain went to war with each other in the spring of that year over events taking place on the Caribbean island nation of Cuba. Americans wanted to give their support to Cuban efforts to overthrow Spain's colonial power.

In anticipation of mounting pressure in the United States to go to war against the Spanish, the U.S. Navy ordered one of its largest battleships, the USS *Oregon*, to steam from San Francisco to Cuba, a distance of twelve thousand miles. To get to Cuba, the *Oregon* had to sail south around South America. The *Oregon* set out on March 19 and arrived at Cuba sixty-seven days later. By then, the Spanish-American War was a month old. Military officials and politicians in the United States had worried that the war in Cuba might be over before the *Oregon* could reach the island.

Although the *Oregon* had arrived in time to take part in the Battle of Santiago Bay, concern about the long trip ran high in the United States. Private citizens and political officeholders ar-gued hotly for an American canal on the isthmus. Leading the charge was a man who in only a few years would be president of the United States: Theodore Roosevelt.

*After a grueling sixty-seven-day journey, the battleship* Oregon *(third from the right) arrives in Cuba in time to participate in the Battle of Santiago Bay. Many Americans were outraged by the long voyage and renewed their demands for an American canal on the isthmus.*

Roosevelt had long supported a U.S. canal on the isthmus. In 1890 he had read a book written by Alfred T. Mahan titled *The Influence of Sea Power on History*. Mahan argued that a powerful and mobile navy was essential to gaining and maintaining a nation's influence overseas. The book had convinced Roosevelt of the same.

As assistant secretary of the navy, he sent letters to members of Congress and to newspaper editors, urging serious thought about an American canal in Central America. After the war his campaign moved into high gear. His typical plea was one given as a speaker before a group of Chicago businessmen:

> If we are to hold our own in the struggle for naval and commercial supremacy, we must build up our power [outside] our borders. We must build the Isthmian canal, and we must grasp the points of vantage which will enable us to have our say in deciding the destiny of the oceans of the east and west.

When word of American interest in an isthmian canal reached the French, they were very excited. The French offered to sell their rights to build a canal in Panama to the Americans for a little over one hundred million dollars. The Americans knew they could negotiate for a lower price, since they were apparently the only interested buyers. The Americans offered the French much less—about forty million dollars. Angered by the low amount, the French rejected the offer.

But the Americans were not to be defeated. Instead of increasing the offer to the French for rights to build a canal in Panama, the U.S. Congress put together a bill that would provide $180 million for the construction of a canal in Nicaragua, one of Panama's northern neighbors.

Now the French were worried. Fearing the loss of their only interested buyer, the French accepted the Americans' forty-million-dollar offer. In turn, Congress abandoned its Nicaraguan canal proposal. In 1899 Congress established the Isthmian Canal Commission. The commission's purpose was to begin organizing an American canal-building effort.

## A NEW TREATY WITH ENGLAND

Before the United States could build a canal on the isthmus, a new treaty with Great Britain had to be negotiated. The nearly fifty-year-old Clayton-Bulwer Treaty required both the United States and Great Britain to share any canal-building project on the isthmus. To the Americans' relief, the British were prepared to give up all rights to an American-built canal in Panama. At the time, Britain was at war in South Africa and did not want the obligation of helping build a canal in Panama or anywhere else.

*Theodore Roosevelt was convinced that an isthmian canal was necessary for the United States to maintain naval supremacy.*

## COLOMBIA HOLDS BACK

By 1902, less than four years after the end of the Spanish-American War, the United States was in position to prepare plans for a canal. But the Americans had overlooked a clause in the original canal-rights contract between the government of Colombia and the French Panama Canal Company. Because Panama was at that time a part of Colombia, Colombia held the rights to the use of that portion of the isthmus. The contract between France and Colombia clearly stated that Colombia had the right to agree or disagree to construction of a canal by someone other than the French Panama Canal Company. Secretary of State John Hay proposed negotiations between Colombia and the United States. After several false starts and delays, Colombia sent Dr. Tomas Herrán, a sixty-year-old Colombian diplomat, to the United States to negotiate.

Negotiations moved slowly. Colombia was concerned that it might lose its control of Panama if the Americans built a canal across the isthmus. The United States had a reputation among many Latin American powers of being a bully and forcing its will in Central and South America. Hay's patience lasted only so long. Finally, on January 21, 1903, Hay told Herrán that if Colombia refused to sign a proposed agreement, the United States would build its canal in Nicaragua instead of Panama.

The next day Herrán met with Hay at the secretary's home and signed the Hay-Herrán Treaty. Three days later Herrán re-

## A NICARAGUAN CANAL?

How close did the United States come to building a canal in the Central American nation of Nicaragua, rather than Panama?

As early as 1826 members of the U.S. Congress had debated the merits of locating a canal across the isthmus in Panama or in Nicaragua, its distant neighbor to the north. After the French shut down their canal building in 1889, three separate U.S. congressional commissions—meeting in 1895, 1897, and 1899—held investigations into the best route for an isthmian canal. Each had determined that any American effort should take place in Nicaragua.

Building a canal in Nicaragua might have had many advantages. Such a canal would be closer than a canal in Panama to any American port by hundreds of miles. The lowest mountain pass in the entire Cordillerian chain from Alaska through South America was located in Nicaragua, which would mean less digging. There were major naviga-

ceived a cable from his superiors in Bogotá. The cable instructed him not to sign the agreement without further instructions. The Colombian government wanted to hold out for more money from the United States. Colombia was also concerned about giving up its sovereignty over any land in Panama where a canal would be built. But it was too late. The treaty had been signed. The Americans were on their way to building the Panama Canal.

## THE HAY-HERRÁN TREATY

Under the new treaty Colombia gave the United States a strip of land across Panama measuring six miles wide. The land covered the canal route the French had spent years working on. It

*U.S. secretary of state John Hay (pictured) successfully negotiated the Hay-Herrán Treaty, which gave the United States the right to build a canal in Panama.*

ble rivers and a great Nicaraguan lake already there for the using. Such natural bodies of water greatly reduced the amount of digging needed for a canal. Six treaties between the United States and Nicaragua were already in existence, together giving the United States permission to build a Nicaraguan canal. And the threat of diseases such as yellow fever and malaria was smaller than in Panama, due to fewer swamps and lowlands.

Supporters of a Panamanian canal had their reasons, too. A Nicaraguan canal would have taken longer to build and would have cost more, too, due to its greater length. President Roosevelt was eventually convinced by American engineers that the Panamanian route was preferable, and his opinion was considered important.

After a long debate was held in the U.S. Senate in the summer of 1902, called the Battle of the Routes, the vote went in favor of a canal in Panama, forty-two to thirty-four.

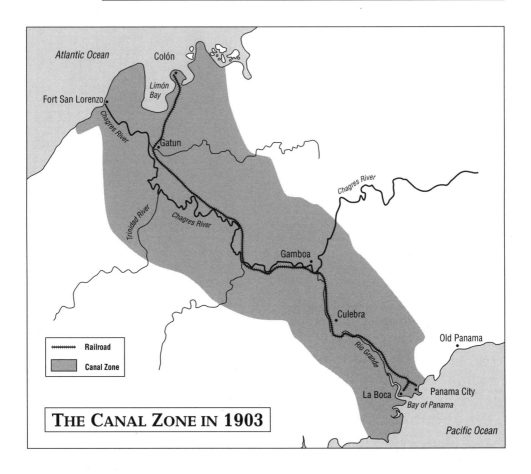

Atlantic Ocean · Colón · Limón Bay · Fort San Lorenzo · Chagres River · Gatun · Trinidad River · Chagres River · Chagres River · Gamboa · Culebra · Old Panama · Rio Grande · La Boca · Panama City · Bay of Panama · Pacific Ocean

Railroad
Canal Zone

THE CANAL ZONE IN 1903

also gave the United States the authority to police the zone and establish Canal Zone courts of law. In exchange, Colombia was to receive $10 million in gold and $250,000 annually for the next hundred years, to begin nine years after the canal opened.

Colombia was not happy with the treaty Herrán had signed. The Colombian congress refused to ratify, or approve, it. Colombians who opposed the treaty demanded that the United States pay twenty-five million dollars: fifteen million dollars to Colombia, and ten million dollars to the French.

Some of the treaty's opponents hit upon a plan for getting more money out of the canal. They planned to delay formal approval until the old agreement between Colombia and the French Panama Canal Company expired. Once that happened, they reasoned, Colombia would receive the forty million dollars the United States was willing to pay the French for canal-building rights, plus the ten million dollars the United States agreed to pay Colombia.

But President Roosevelt and the people of Panama saw things differently. Roosevelt felt the treaty had been negotiated in good faith and that Colombia was simply holding out for more money. The people of Panama, who had been little more than onlookers in this whole episode, appeared to want the Americans to build a canal.

In October 1903 the Colombian congress adjourned without ratifying the Hay-Herrán Treaty. Many in Panama were furious with the politicians in Bogotá. The possibility of a Panamanian canal was quickly slipping away. The time seemed right for the Panamanians to take events into their own hands.

## REVOLUTION IN PANAMA!

The idea of a Panamanian revolution against Colombia was nothing new. Panama had twice tried to separate from Colombia, first in 1841, and again in 1853. But Colombian troops had always put down any attempt by Panamanians to win their independence. This time, however, Panama had a powerful ally. The United States was prepared to help Panama in its quest for independence.

On October 30, 1903, President Roosevelt, in support of the Panamanian revolution, dispatched the *Nashville*, a U.S. Navy cruiser, from Jamaica to Colón, Panama. Three days later the *Nashville* reached its destination. Later that same day, a Colombian gunboat, the *Cartagena*, steamed into Colón Harbor, where the *Nashville* lay waiting.

The next few days were tension filled as Panamanian revolutionaries and U.S. naval officers insisted that the Colombians sail out of Colón. Other

*To show his support for the Panamanian revolution, President Roosevelt sent the navy cruiser* Nashville *to aid in the fight for independence from Colombia.*

American and Colombian naval ships arrived at Colón, adding to the drama. At one point the *Nashville* actually moved into position near the *Cartagena* and aimed its guns at the Colombian vessel. There was no exchange of gunfire, but the

*Nashville's* presence had achieved its purpose. The Colombians ordered their vessel home, and the *Cartagena* left Colón.

President Roosevelt expressed delight at the news of the Colombian withdrawal. On November 6, 1903, at 11:35 in the morning, word came from Panama City that the new Republic of Panama had been established. Less than two weeks later the United States signed a treaty with Panama, preparing the way for a canal.

## ENTER PHILIPPE BUNAU-VARILLA

The man responsible for negotiating this treaty for Panama was not a Panamanian. He was a French citizen who had worked as an engineer for the Panama Canal Company but had not seen Panama in eighteen years. His name was Philippe Bunau-Varilla. At the time of the Panamanian revolution, he was an agent of the French New Panama Canal Company, which had been formed in 1894 when the old company went broke. Before 1894 Bunau-Varilla had worked as an engineer of the old company and held a large amount of stock in the new company. Bunau-Varilla, through his agents in Panama, had helped organize the Panamanian revolution against Colombia, providing them with money, a proclamation of independence, a draft of a constitution, and a flag design for the new republic. He had kept Roosevelt and Hay informed of the plans for the revolution. Information from Bunau-Varilla had led Roosevelt to send the *Nashville* to Colón in the first place.

*Following the Panamanian revolution, French diplomat Philippe Bunau-Varilla skillfully negotiated the Hay–Bunau-Varilla Treaty between the United States and the newly independent nation of Panama.*

The new treaty negotiated by Bunau-Varilla was a simple one, called the Hay–Bunau-Varilla Treaty. In many ways, it resembled the Hay-Herrán Treaty. As with the agreement with Colombia, the United States was to pay Panama $10 million immediately and $250,000 annually "in perpetuity," meaning forever. The payments would take effect nine years after the

## OF VOLCANOES AND POSTAGE STAMPS

Without a doubt Philippe Bunau-Varilla played an important role in seeing that the U.S. Senate voted for a Panamanian canal rather than a canal in Nicaragua. And sometimes his tactics were shady, indeed.

Most importantly, he wrote and published thirteen thousand copies of a pamphlet entitled *Panama or Nicaragua?* in which he listed the advantages of building in Panama. Bunau-Varilla sent copies of the pamphlet to every American congressman, to every state governor, and to thousands of American bankers, shipowners, financiers, and newspaper editors.

Among the chief disadvantages he listed for a Nicaraguan canal was the threat of volcanic eruptions.

To emphasize his point, just days before the U.S. Senate was scheduled to vote on a canal site, Bunau-Varilla sent all the senators one last message. He had searched in stamp dealer shops all over Washington, D.C., for a one-centavo Nicaraguan stamp that he remembered, which pictured a railroad dock with an active volcano in the background, smoke pouring from its cone.

Finding ninety such stamps, just the number he needed, he stuck each one on separate sheets of paper and typed these words below: "An official witness of the volcanic activity on the isthmus of Nicaragua." Senators found the stamps in their morning mail on Monday, June 16, 1902, just three days before the important vote.

How much difference did the postage stamps make in the Senate's final decision? Probably little. However, Bunau-Varilla's pamphlet, with its volcanic warnings, certainly caused more senators to support a Panamanian canal.

But what most Senators did not know was that nearly all of Nicaragua's fourteen volcanoes were already extinct and that the few that had shown any sign of activity, even in recent centuries, were many miles from where a canal would have been constructed. Bunau-Varilla's threat of Nicaraguan volcanoes, therefore, was largely just so much smoke.

canal was completed and opened. However, the new treaty also differed from the old one. The Hay-Herrán Treaty had allowed for a one hundred-year lease. And the six-mile-wide zone agreed to in the treaty with Colombia became a ten-mile-wide zone in the treaty with Panama. Also, the French were free to transfer their rights and property, including the Panama Railroad Company, to the United States.

Once Secretary of State Hay and Bunau-Varilla signed the treaty, the Frenchman worked hard to make certain that the Panamanian legislature ratified it. He used many different tactics, some questionable. On November 25 he sent a cablegram to Panama, warning government leaders that if Panama did not ratify the treaty soon, the Americans would remove their offer and make a deal with the Colombians. This was a bluff.

Ratification of the treaty by both nations was accomplished in three months. The provisional government of Panama approved the treaty unanimously and with no changes. The U.S. Senate approved the treaty on February 23, 1904, but after much bitter debate. Some senators felt the U.S. government had supported the Panamanian revolution just to get a favorable canal treaty from Panama. Mississippi senator Hernando de Soto Money noted that the treaty gave "us more than anybody in this Chamber ever dreamed of having . . . we have never had a concession so extraordinary in its character as this. In fact, it sounds very much as if we wrote it ourselves."

## CONTROVERSY OVER THE TREATY

Many questions and criticisms still exist about Bunau-Varilla and the authority he had to negotiate such a treaty with the United States. Just days after he signed the treaty, supposedly on Panama's behalf, representatives of the new Panamanian government arrived in Washington ready to negotiate. They were disappointed to discover that Bunau-Varilla had already signed a treaty.

Critics of Bunau-Varilla have argued that he did not make the treaty in Panama's self-interest but to help the French Panama Canal Company, in which he had invested $440,000. Ratification of the treaty by the United States and Panama meant that the Panama Canal Company would receive $40 million for their rights to the canal. Only then did Bunau-Varilla recover his $440,000 investment, plus a small profit. But

Bunau-Varilla always claimed to be motivated by loftier goals—in particular, his allegiance to France. After making the treaty, Bunau-Varilla said: "I have fulfilled my mission. . . . I have safeguarded the work of the French genius; I have avenged its honor; I have served France."

Additional controversy focused on President Roosevelt. During debate on the treaty, some senators were critical of President Roosevelt and his role in pushing along the Panamanian revolution for his own political purposes. But most Americans were unconcerned with such accusations. The United States had permission to build a canal in Panama. Roosevelt was seen as a hero to many in the United States. Too many years had passed since the French were busily at work carving their way across the isthmus. Now it was the job of the United States to take up where the French left off, and, in the words of the excitable Theodore Roosevelt, "let the dirt fly!"

# 3

# WALLACE AND STEVENS LEAD THE WAY

The French had spent many years working on a canal across the fifty-mile-long Isthmus of Panama. But they had failed. When the Americans took over the immense project in 1904, they soon discovered a tremendous task ahead of them.

## SELECTING A CHIEF ENGINEER

Roosevelt selected a seven-man Isthmian Canal Commission to oversee the project. The seven commissioners sailed to Panama

*The Isthmian Canal Commission selected railroad engineer John F. Wallace to head the project. Despite his overwhelming fear of yellow fever, Wallace accepted the job and headed for Panama.*

in the spring of 1904 to inspect the proposed canal route. Once there, they had to make important decisions. One decision was whether to build a sea-level canal or one that required locks. Although the commissioners had no real understanding of the work and cost involved in a sea-level canal, they chose it over a canal with locks. They also planned to use the same route the French had worked on. Finally, they picked as chief engineer John F. Wallace, a longtime Chicago railroad man and a former president of the American Society of Civil Engineers. He had built rail lines and terminals for the Illinois Central Railroad.

Wallace accepted the job after much hesitation. Although his salary was set at twenty-five thousand dollars a year, a hefty sum in those days, it did not allay many of Wallace's fears, including his greatest: contracting yellow fever in the hot, sticky Pana-

*When the French abandoned the canal project, the equipment they left behind became covered by vines and undergrowth. Valuable steam shovels and locomotives (pictured) were rendered useless by the lush Panamanian jungle.*

manian jungle. Wallace was so afraid that he would die of the disease that he brought to Panama two elaborate metal coffins, one for himself and one for his wife. Wallace also feared that the commission members would have problems agreeing on how the canal work should progress. These men did their work from Washington, D.C. Wallace was concerned that his labors in Panama might be hampered by a commission out of touch with the on-the-job realities of canal work.

## WHAT THE FRENCH LEFT BEHIND

Although neither he nor his wife contracted yellow fever, the lush jungle made Wallace's job more difficult than he might have imagined. When Wallace arrived in the Canal Zone in 1904, he found what could only be described as a mess. The Panamanian jungle had grown over much of the work site. Wallace had hoped to use equipment left behind by the French, but most of it was unusable. Vines and undergrowth covered rusty locomotives, steam shovels, and other equipment.

Many of the buildings erected for housing and offices were falling apart. Wallace realized there was much work ahead. He described his initial impressions of the scene in Panama as "jungle and chaos from one end of the Isthmus to the other."

It would take an army of workers to put the work site back into operation. His men would also have to work hard to make Panama liveable for what promised to be a long stay.

## A DIFFICULT FIRST YEAR

Life was very difficult that first year in Panama. Fresh water was hard to come by during the dry season, which lasted from about mid-December through April. The housing was poor, with five or six workers sharing a small room. The food was, perhaps, the worst. Many workers survived for weeks on canned sardines, crackers, and salted, canned butter. Fresh milk and vegetables were not available. Men became sick from the living conditions. Many of the first workers quit and went home.

*Workers take a break from their labors to cook a quick meal along the railroad tracks. Poor living and working conditions made the first year in Panama difficult for most workers.*

On their return they spoke of the poor living and working conditions in the Canal Zone. Newspapers ran a copy of a letter sent by a worker to his mother in Pittsburgh: "Tell the boys to stay home if they get only a dollar a day. Everybody is afflicted with running sores. . . . The meals would sicken a dog."

Disgusted workers returning from Panama also described how little digging was being done. Some accused Wallace of wasting money and accomplishing little.

Work on the canal did move along slowly that first year. Wallace was a hard worker and tried his best to make progress, but he faced many problems. For one thing, he was often slowed down by bureaucratic rules and regulations. All his orders for machinery, tools, equipment, or anything else had to be approved by the chairman of the commission, Admiral John

G. Walker. Walker studied each purchase order from Wallace to make certain that what was ordered was really needed. He also wanted to make sure that no one was trying to cheat the government. It was not that Walker did not trust Wallace. He was just a cautious man. Walker knew there had been much dishonesty when the French worked on the canal.

The result was that many of Wallace's orders were held up for months at a time. Some of his orders for equipment went to companies that boasted of low prices but then failed to come through with the needed equipment.

## ROOSEVELT SHAKES THINGS UP

The lack of progress did not look good to the American public. Ever mindful of public opinion, Roosevelt became dissatisfied with the slow rate of progress on the canal. He was unhappy with the way the seven-man canal commission was working and decided to put an end to it.

Roosevelt did hold on to Wallace, however. Wallace retained his job as chief engineer and joined the new, three-man commission that the president appointed on April 1, 1905.

*Spectators survey the digging of the Panama Canal in this 1905 photograph. In the valley below, busy steam shovels excavate the trench.*

Wallace hoped his position on the new commission would speed up work on the canal. But he was soon disappointed. Although Wallace held one of the three seats on the commission, the other two commissioners gave him nearly as many problems as had the previous seven.

Weary of the constant conflict between himself and the other members of the commission, Wallace met with Secretary of War William Howard Taft in New York in June 1905. Historian W. Leon Pepperman's book *Who Built the Panama Canal?*, published just a year after the canal was finished, offers a detailed description of the Taft-Wallace meeting. According to Pepperman, Wallace threatened to resign his position unless Taft agreed to make him chairman of the canal commission and give him full authority over the canal project. He also wanted his salary to be raised to sixty thousand dollars.

Angered by Wallace's threat, Secretary Taft immediately accepted the chief engineer's resignation. Taft reminded Wallace that his salary was already ten thousand dollars more than that of the French chief engineer before him. He also informed Wallace that the chief engineer had understood the challenge of the canal project before he took the job. According to Pepperman, Taft told Wallace:

> I am inexpressibly disappointed, not only because you have taken this step, but because you seem so utterly insensible of the significance of your conduct. . . . For mere lucre [money] you change your position overnight. . . . You are influenced solely by your personal advantage. . . . I do not consider that any man can divide such a duty up to any one point where it suits him to stop. . . . In my view a duty is an entirety and is not fulfilled unless it is wholly fulfilled.

Within just a few days of Wallace's resignation, Roosevelt appointed a replacement. He picked a man he had never met and knew very little about: John Frank Stevens.

## A NEW CHIEF ENGINEER

Stevens was recommended first to Taft, then to Roosevelt, by one of America's great railroad builders, James J. Hill. Stevens had been one of Hill's building engineers. Although he had little experience building canals and much experience building railroads, he was just what the Panama Canal project needed.

John Stevens was fifty-two years old in 1905, average in height but powerfully built. He was a handsome man with a dark complexion and a thick black mustache. He grew up on a farm in Maine and became a surveyor. In 1873 Stevens went west, helping to survey the new city of Minneapolis. He also spent his young years working on the new railroads in Minnesota and Texas, where he drove railroad spikes for $1.10 a day. Eventually he became an assistant engineer, helping to build at least six different western rail lines, including the Canadian Pacific.

By the time he was called to work on the Panama Canal in 1905, Stevens was a vice president of the Chicago,

*After Wallace resigned, President Roosevelt selected John Frank Stevens (pictured) as the new chief engineer.*

Rock Island, and Pacific Railroad, one of the first large midwestern railroads. At first Stevens did not want the new job. But his wife talked him into it, telling him that his entire career had led him to this great engineering challenge.

## A "DEVIL OF A MESS"

Just three weeks after Wallace resigned, Stevens met with President Roosevelt at Oyster Bay on New York's Long Island, a favorite vacation spot for the president. Roosevelt explained to Stevens that the project in Panama was in a "devil of a mess."

Stevens had decided ahead of time that he would take the job only if Roosevelt agreed to certain conditions. Most importantly, Stevens told Roosevelt, he did not want anyone trying to tell him how to do his job, including congressmen, the War Department, and the canal commission. Roosevelt heartily agreed. He even told Stevens to skip reporting to the canal commission altogether and report directly to him.

At this meeting both Roosevelt and Stevens revealed how important it was to each of them that the Panama Canal be completed soon. Before the meeting ended, the two men shook

## STEVENS DISCOVERS MARIAS PASS

John Frank Stevens's life was as colorful as he was capable. In 1889 he went to work for James J. Hill, the great western railroad tycoon. Before the year was over, Stevens was legendary among railroad builders.

In Montana he won fame by rediscovering the Marias Pass through the Rocky Mountains. The pass had been discovered by the early-nineteenth-century explorers Lewis and Clark, lost, then rediscovered fifty years later by surveyors, and lost again. Hill sent Stevens to find the pass. For months, Stevens searched. He finally found the pass in the dead of winter.

Trapped by blizzard conditions, Stevens's Indian guide left him when the temperature hit forty degrees below zero. Stevens kept himself alive by pacing back and forth in the heavy snows several nights in a row to avoid freezing. Rediscovering the pass saved Hill over one hundred miles of railroad construction. The pass lies today in Glacier National Park. Stevens was honored years later with the erection of a statue in Summit, Montana, on the very location of the campsite where he nearly froze to death.

*Long before John Frank Stevens became Panama's chief engineer, his exploits in Montana's Marias Pass made him a legend among railroad builders.*

hands in agreement. Roosevelt told Stevens that he was reminded of the story about the man who hired a butler, saying to him: "I don't know in the least what you are to do, but you get busy and buttle like hell!" Roosevelt had his new chief engineer. Within a week Stevens was on his way to Panama.

### STEVENS SIZES UP THE SITUATION

What Stevens found in Panama was just what President Roosevelt had described to him: a devil of a mess. The Atlantic port city of Colón and Panama City, on the opposite shore of Panama, were filthy places, offering bad drinking water and terrible food. The streets of the two cities were littered with waste and garbage. The fear of disease was everywhere, especially of yellow fever. When Stevens's ship docked at Colón, dozens of canal workers met him at the wharf. They were not there to greet their new boss. They were preparing to leave, fed up with the poor working and living conditions in the Canal Zone.

Once ashore, Stevens found more problems. Government regulations slowed down nearly all work on the canal. For example, carpenters could not cut a board longer than ten feet without a written permit. Getting a handcart required signatures on six different documents. As Stevens moved into the interior to inspect the canal work, he discovered that every steam shovel on the canal was idle. He watched as two new canal workers from the Caribbean island of Martinique filled a wheelbarrow with dirt, then placed it on the head of a third worker, who carried the load off that way. Nothing was really getting accomplished. When Stevens arrived on the scene, many of the workers assumed he was there to tell them all that the project was to be abandoned and that they were all going home. But Stevens had big plans for everyone in the Canal Zone.

*In Colón, a man tries to fish his hat from a muddy road while passersby look on. Workers endured polluted drinking water, appalling food, and the ever-present threat of disease in both Colón and Panama City.*

## A NEW STRATEGY

First, Stevens went to work at boosting the workers' morale. Rather than sit behind a desk, out of sight of the common workers, Stevens put on overalls and rubber boots and tromped up and down the zone. The workers began at once to feel as if he was one of them. In a short time Stevens surveyed the entire route of the canal, roughly following the old French route. But work on the canal did not speed up. In fact, the new chief engineer sent nearly all the steam shovel and heavy machinery operators back to the United States. He said he would send for them later. He put the remaining crews to work on improving living conditions. Within six months decent and clean housing, mess halls, schools, and hospitals rose in the Canal Zone.

*Workers pause to pose for this 1905 photograph. When Stevens took charge of the project, he tried to improve the workers' morale and productivity.*

Despite such improvements in living conditions, the workers still had one major complaint: boredom. One young worker wrote a letter to the *New York Herald*: "There is not a bit of amusement or pleasure of the remotest kind here. . . . It is a case of work, work, work, all day long, and infrequently all night long."

To make life in the zone more bearable, Stevens had the men build churches, clubhouses, and bandstands. Eventually an orchestra could be heard playing in the jungles of the Canal Zone. The men constructed baseball fields. Each worker settlement along the line was to get up a baseball team for sport competition. When told by a young clerk that there was no money available for field construction, Stevens told him to charge the costs to sanitary expenses.

Twelve thousand workers spent at least six months not digging along the canal route, but building a sewage disposal facility and new docks in the harbor. Stevens ordered a telephone and telegraph system built, using old railroad ties for poles.

*A teacher and her students gather for a portrait at the Canal Zone Free Public School.*

Stevens also had refrigeration equipment shipped to the Canal Zone. For the first time the canal workers could dine on fresh meats, eggs, and vegetables in every season. Soon Stevens had convinced nearly all the workers to stay. He inspired his workers, telling them: "There are three diseases on the Isthmus: yellow fever, malaria, and cold feet. And the worst of these is cold feet."

## STEVENS BRINGS MORE CHANGES

Not long after landing in Panama, Stevens made what could be described as his most important decision. This one concerned the canal itself. Rather than continuing with the sea-level canal, started by the first canal commission, Stevens set his mind on a lock canal. In his memoirs, *An Engineer's Recollections*, Stevens described his reasons for supporting a lock canal: "It will provide a safer and quicker passage for ships. . . . Its cost of operation, maintenance and fixed charges will be much less than any sea-level canal." Stevens also argued that the lock canal would require much less digging, for ships could be lifted up the canal through a series of locks. He estimated that a lock canal could be completed in nine years, while he

## GOLD ROLLS AND RACIAL ROLES

Workers in the Canal Zone came from all corners of the world. Under the Americans, as previously under the French, ninety-seven different nations were represented by the engineers, workers, and common laborers. Some jobs required specific skills; others required nothing more than a pick, a shovel, and a strong back.

All workers hired in the Canal Zone were given a contract that guaranteed them free passage to Panama. Much of the unskilled labor came from the black population of the West Indies island of Jamaica. These black workers found not only hard work in the Canal Zone, but racism, as well.

Segregation was firmly in place there, as it was back in the United States. Black workers had separate mess halls, housing, schools, and hospitals. The Panama Railroad was loosely segregated into first- and second-class railcars, with blacks expected to ride in the second-class cars. However, low-paid white laborers often rode in the second-class cars, and skilled blacks sometimes could be found in first-class seats.

Some discrimination was disguised. Although official Canal Zone rules and regulations might not mention black and white, they did refer to gold and silver. This was a reference to the pay system in the Canal Zone. Unskilled, often black, workers were paid in Panamanian silver balboas. White foreign workers, even the skilled ones, were also paid in silver. White American workers were paid in gold, then the monetary standard in the United States. So, the gold and silver payrolls was one general way of treating the workers differently, with non-American and black American workers receiving less pay for their efforts.

*Canal workers crowd into separate gold and silver lines as the payroll car makes a stop at Culebra on January 12, 1908.*

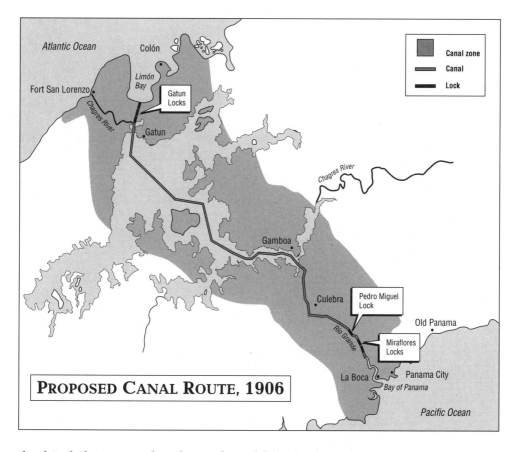

**PROPOSED CANAL ROUTE, 1906**

doubted that a sea-level canal could be built in fewer than eighteen years, if at all.

Once Stevens had made up his mind, he had to convince the canal commission, President Roosevelt, and Congress. On February 5, 1906, the Isthmian Canal Commission agreed with Stevens that a lock canal was necessary. Within weeks President Roosevelt was also convinced. But Congress was still determined to see that a sea-level canal was built.

In May, Stevens appeared before the House Committee on Interstate and Foreign Commerce. He told the committee that "the one great problem in the construction of any canal down there [in Panama] is the control of the Chagres River. That overshadows everything else." The Chagres was a wild river that flooded often during the rainy season. If not contained, the Chagres would pose a constant threat to a sea-level canal, which would have to be cut across the path of the river. Stevens argued

*A giant steam shovel loads railroad cars with dirt and rock in this photograph from 1905.*

that a total of six double locks was needed for the canal, with each lock requiring gigantic steel gates. A lock was to be built at the south end of the Culebra Cut, near the village of Pedro Miguel, site of a secondary-level lake, and two additional locks at Sosa Hill. On the Atlantic side the three Gatun Locks would be built, leading ships to Gatun Lake, which would be created once the planned Gatun Dam harnessed the Chagres River. The Panamanian jungle would surround the locks, the lake, and Culebra Cut. Finally, on June 21, the Senate voted thirty-six to thirty-one for the construction of a lock canal.

The decision to build a lock canal was an important step. It meant much less excavation work for the canal crews. While the route remained largely the same as had been planned for a sea-level canal, the digging at Culebra Mountain alone was cut in half, from an estimated 230 million cubic yards of earth to 105 million cubic yards.

Even with the decision to build a lock canal, much work lay ahead for Stevens and his men. To build the canal would require much heavy equipment for digging and a good railroad to haul out the dirt and rock and to transport supplies and equipment. The old Panama Railroad had to be rebuilt and its track doubled. Stevens ordered more than eighty ninety-five-ton Bucyrus steam shovels, the largest in the world. In addition, he had eight hundred flatcars and over one hundred locomotives, hundreds of rock drills, and thousands of hand tools shipped into the Canal Zone. Everything was soon in place to do exactly what President Roosevelt had wanted in the zone all along: "make the dirt fly."

## STEVENS MAKES HIS REPUTATION

The workers under Stevens's leadership soon came to respect him, considering him a fair man and a capable and intelligent engineer. But Stevens was also a hard worker, often putting in twelve- and fourteen-hour days. He expected as much from his crews as he did from himself. Anything less was unacceptable.

When Stevens first arrived in the zone, he was shown the plans for a grand house to be built for him at Panama Bay. He said no. Stevens wanted to be near the work sites. He ordered work crews to build a small house with a corrugated tin roof on the side of Culebra Cut, where much of the digging took place. As the weeks and months passed, Stevens was on the job, working closely with his crews, giving orders, making progress. Always puffing on big cigars, Stevens was soon known by his men as Big Smoke.

Once the work and living environment of the Canal Zone had been improved, Stevens turned his full attention to building the canal. Stevens saw building the canal as a two-part problem: the digging itself and disposing of the dirt, rock, and slate from the canal site. As a railroad man, he determined that an extensive network of railroads was the answer to the disposal problem. Historian David McCullough, writing in his book *The Path Between the Seas*, describes Stevens's approach:

> Stevens' objective was to create a system of dirt trains that would function like a colossal conveyor belt, rolling endlessly beside steam shovels working at several levels at once. . . . [Stevens] would haul the dirt to either coast, or to both, or to wherever it was needed for fill. . . . Culebra could supply the material to build the necessary dams. By double-tracking the railroad he had provided open access in both directions without interrupting regular traffic on the line. The distance from the point of excavation to the dumping grounds was

immaterial. It made no difference whether the dirt had to be moved ten feet or ten miles. The trick was to keep the dirt trains in constant motion in and out of the Cut, to and from the dumps.

Following this plan, work progressed quickly. The first month, work crews removed 70,630 yards of slate, clay, and rock from Culebra Cut. They hauled out another 120,000 yards the following month. Six months later, the steam shovel operators were taking out almost 250,000 yards a month. Stevens was moving mountains.

While work at Culebra progressed, construction of Gatun Dam was underway. The dam was being designed to control the usually raging Chagres River, which cut across the canal's route. Rail tracks were being laid to the site. Once the dam was

*John Stevens (right) worked closely with his crewmen and quickly gained their respect. Under Stevens's able supervision, laborers continued to make headway in the Culebra Cut and elsewhere.*

## COLONEL GORGAS'S CAMPAIGN AGAINST YELLOW FEVER

While the Canal Zone, especially the Culebra Cut, was busy with the racket of puffing, creaking steam shovels and clattering railroad cars, Colonel William Crawford Gorgas, a medical doctor and the chief sanitary officer, was busy quietly fighting a battle against disease. His mission: to eliminate the threat of yellow fever and malaria from all of Panama.

Europeans and Americans were especially vulnerable to these diseases, which were spread by mosquitoes. Many Panamanian natives, other Caribbean peoples, and blacks in general found themselves largely immune to yellow fever and malaria. But whites caught both diseases easily and in large numbers. The diseases had hampered the canal-building efforts of the French, and by 1904 a serious outbreak of yellow fever was sweeping through the Canal Zone. Each month scores of canal workers became sick with yellow fever, and several died.

*Col. William Crawford Gorgas*

Gorgas identified mosquitoes as the carriers of the deadly diseases. This theory had been known for several decades, but many medical doctors questioned its validity. Gorgas led a health campaign against the dreaded fevers.

He sent his men throughout the zone, fumigating each house and shop. Standing pools of water were sprayed with kerosene, and ditches were drained to eliminate the mosquitoes' breeding sites. Under Stevens, all new buildings were protected with wire screening to keep out the pesky mosquitoes. Gorgas's original medical budget was fifty thousand dollars. Stevens himself would sign requisitions for ninety thousand dollars in window and door screening alone.

Through Gorgas's efforts, the last case of yellow fever was reported in December 1905.

in place, it would rein in the Chagres River, creating Gatun Lake. The lake was to cover 164 square miles of Panamanian rain forest. Gatun Lake was important to those building the canal. When the locks were completed later at both ends of the canal, ships would be raised up to the lake where they would steam through the man-made, inland waters.

## A VISIT FROM THE PRESIDENT

Word of the progress being made on the canal reached the highest levels of American government. In November 1906 President Roosevelt sailed to Panama on the battleship *Louisiana* to see for himself what his new chief engineer had accomplished. Arriving in the Canal Zone, Roosevelt discovered just what he was hoping for: progress. As Stevens had done, Roosevelt tromped all over the work site, talking to the

*Overflowing with soil and rock, dirt cars work side by side with mighty excavators in the canal site. An extensive network of railroads quickly transported dirt from the trench to nearby dump sites, solving the problem of disposal.*

*During his visit to Panama, President Roosevelt explored the work site in depth. This 1906 photograph shows the adventurous president aboard one of the many steam shovels at work in Culebra Cut.*

chief engineer, eating the same food the workers ate. Clearly Roosevelt was pleased with the work Stevens had completed. In a speech to the workers in the Canal Zone, Roosevelt said: "You, here, who do your work well in bringing to completion this great enterprise, will stand exactly as the soldiers of a few, and only a few of the most famous armies of all the nations stand in history."

After three days in the zone, President Roosevelt left Panama with the same full confidence in Stevens he had had nearly eighteen months earlier. Stevens was his man, and Roosevelt was certain he would get the canal finished. Little did the President know that within three months of his visit to Panama, Stevens was to announce he was leaving.

# 4

# GOETHALS COMPLETES THE JOB

When Stevens resigned as chief engineer, he gave no explanation for his decision, nor would he ever tell his reasons. Stevens's resignation hit America's canal project like a landslide in Culebra Cut. President Roosevelt was furious. He had now lost two chief engineers, and he was determined not to lose a third. "I propose now to put it [construction of the canal] in charge of men who will stay on the job until I get tired of having them there, or till I say they may abandon it. I shall turn it over to the Army." He picked a capable officer in the Army Corps of Engineers, Colonel George Washington Goethals.

Colonel George Washington Goethals became the third and final chief engineer to work on the Panama Canal project.

## AN ARMY MAN TAKES COMMAND

Colonel Goethals was considered a model soldier. By age forty-eight he had served in the engineering corps for over twenty years. Friends and associates described the trim, six-foot-tall soldier as proper, serious, and demanding.

Roosevelt selected Goethals not just for his general experience in engineering, but because the colonel had firsthand experience with the Panama Canal. He had visited the canal project in 1905 with Secretary of War William Howard Taft. In fact, it was Taft who suggested Goethals to Roosevelt when Stevens resigned.

## DYNAMITE: A DEADLY TOOL

Over thirty thousand tons of dynamite were used to excavate the route of the Panamanian canal. These explosives represented more destructive energy than had been fired in all the wars the United States had ever fought before World War I. Half the laborers on the canal worked, in some way, at some time, with dynamite.

Two types of drills were used to set the dynamite charges: one could bore a five-inch-wide hole to a depth of one hundred feet, while the other could drill a three-inch-diameter hole thirty feet deep. The Americans used compressed air to power these drills, which ran from large compressors located miles away.

Many accidents with explosives occurred. Goethals himself was not in the zone long before he noted: "We are having too many accidents with blasts. One killed 9 men on Thursday at Pedro Miguel. The foreman blown all to pieces."

Although great care was generally taken in handling the explosives, mistakes and accidents were never eliminated. Dynamite exploded on several occasions when

*Using long poles, workers carefully load dynamite into predrilled holes.*

workers' shovels hit and detonated a dynamite cap. One twelve-ton blast occurred when lightning struck the charge, killing seven workers.

On December 12, 1908, at Bas Obispo, the worst single dynamite accident took place. A crew had just finished setting fifty charge holes on the west bank of the cut. They had loaded the holes with twenty-two tons of dynamite. All was ready but the wiring, which was to take place at five o'clock. As two workers finished setting the final charge, the entire set of charges exploded. The blast killed twenty-three workers and injured nearly forty more. No cause for the explosion was ever discovered.

Years later Berisford Mitchell, a West Indian worker, made a gruesome note about the loss of life through dynamite explosions: "The flesh of men flew in the air like birds many days."

When Roosevelt made his offer to the colonel, he offered Goethals a free rein in running the project. Roosevelt told him to ignore the canal commission's interferences and report directly to the president. Roosevelt emphasized to the army engineer his impatience with further construction delays. "The Canal must be built!" said the president. Goethals took the words as a direct order from his commander in chief.

## ARRIVING IN PANAMA

Goethals arrived in Panama in March 1907 along with two army engineers, Majors David De Bose Gaillard and William L. Sibert. Sibert was to direct the Atlantic division of the project, and Gaillard was to oversee work in the central division, where Culebra Cut was located.

Goethals at first was not popular among the workers in the Canal Zone. They worried that this army man might try to impose military rule on them or make other changes that would make their lives miserable. But Goethals had no intention of making changes, at least not right away. He even stated this publicly when a reporter asked what he intended to change now that he was in charge. Goethals's answer was a relief to many: "No changes whatsoever will be made in this splendid organization."

## LOOKING OVER THE SITUATION

A couple of years had passed since Goethals had visited the Canal, and what he saw upon his arrival astonished him. So much had been accomplished by Stevens and his workers. Goethals later wrote:

> The people talk about the success of the Army engineer at Panama, but it was fortunate that Mr. Stevens preceded us. The real problem of digging the Canal had been the disposal of the spoil and no Army engineer in America could have laid out the transportation scheme as Mr. Stevens did. We are building on the foundation he laid, and the world can not give him too much credit.

But for all Stevens had accomplished, there was still plenty of work to do. Excavation was under way, especially at Culebra Cut, but still only in its early stages. Some of the canal route surveys were not even complete. Questions about the dimen-

*Chief engineer Goethals (in white) proved to be an efficient supervisor. To manage the thirty thousand workers under him, Goethals traveled throughout the canal site in his yellow-roofed railroad car, nicknamed the "Yellow Peril" (pictured).*

sions and even the locations of some of the canal locks were still unanswered. Work on the canal's most complex features— Gatun Dam, the massive locks, the tremendous digging project in Culebra Cut—had either barely begun or was still in the planning stage.

Although Stevens had retained his position as chairman of the canal commission after leaving his post as chief engineer, he also gave up that position shortly after Goethals's arrival. Goethals took over as commission chairman, making him more powerful in the Canal Zone than anyone except Secretary Taft and President Roosevelt. As commission chairman, Goethals had no other superiors to report to. No wonder he was soon referred to as the Czar of the Zone.

Such control was necessary for any chief engineer in the Canal Zone. Before the end of 1907 the canal project employed thirty thousand workers. This vast workforce required organization, direction, and discipline to make their efforts result in efficient progress. Goethals provided all of these and proved to be the man for the job.

## EATING IN THE CANAL ZONE ON THIRTY CENTS

Bringing thousands of workers to the Canal Zone meant having to provide food for them all. Eventually the Americans established four different kinds of eating establishments: the large Tivoli Hotel, at least twenty line hotels, Spanish or European messes, and West Indian laborers' kitchens.

The Tivoli was a half-million-dollar facility for American engineers and other well-paid employees who wished to live in a modern hotel. Meals here ran between three and three and a half dollars a day, more than the average canal laborer made in a day's work.

The line hotels were not really hotels at all, but great dining rooms where American workers could eat for thirty cents a meal. Non-Americans had to pay fifty cents each. For their thirty or fifty cents, diners were offered a daily menu that was guaranteed to please. A typical lunch, served at one of the line hotels called the Cristobal Hotel, consisted of all the following: vegetable soup, fried pork chops, applesauce, boiled potatoes, pork and beans, sliced buttered beets, stewed cranberries, creamed parsnips, lemon meringue pie, tea, coffee, and cocoa. Supper was even more elaborate: consommé vermicelli, beefsteak, natural gravy, lyonnaise potatoes, stewed beans, sliced beets, stewed apples, julienne carrots, hot biscuits, ice cream, chocolate cake, tea, coffee, and cocoa.

Messes for the European workers—often called Spanish messes, because many European workers were Spaniards—offered a more limited menu of stewed meat, potatoes, cabbage, and bread. West Indian workers were fed American regular army field rations, which consisted of stewed beef, boiled potatoes, navy beans, porridge, rice, and bananas. Such meals were never popular with the West Indian workers.

## GOETHALS MAKES CHANGES

Despite Goethals's original guarantee to make "no changes whatsoever," change did take place. During his first year on the job, alterations were made in the basic plan of the canal. Goethals knew that the United States had designed a new, 98-foot-wide battleship—to be called the USS *Pennsylvania*—that would not fit through the canal in its present size. So Goethals decided to widen Culebra Cut and ordered the lock chambers enlarged from a width of 95 feet to 110 feet.

While some aspects of the canal design were being changed, others went under construction as originally planned.

At the Pacific entrance to the canal, engineers began building a three-mile-long breakwater. The breakwater's purpose was to keep the sand-carrying tidal currents from clogging the canal's entrance. Also, the proposed sites for the canal's Pacific locks were changed. In addition to the planned Pedro Miguel lock south of the Culebra Cut, a second set of locks was designed for a site farther inland at Miraflores. The purpose of the change was to make enemy bombardment from a ship more difficult by placing the locks away from the coast.

During the Goethals years the work on the Panama Canal reached its peak. The real center of attention in the Canal Zone continued to be Culebra Cut, where six thousand men toiled daily. Work on the cut stretched on for seven years. One visitor described the work in this immense canyon, which, when finished in 1913, would measure 300 feet wide at its narrowest, have an average depth of 120 feet, and extend for nine

*Dynamite is loaded into holes in the west bank of Culebra Cut, where some six thousand workers forged a path through the great Culebra mountain range.*

miles in length: "He who did not see the Culebra Cut during the mighty work of excavation missed one of the great spectacles of the ages—a sight that no other time, or place was, or will be, given to man to see."

## SIGHTS AND SOUNDS AT CULEBRA

Old photographs of the work at Culebra Cut provide an idea of the size of the construction work and the height of the mountain. But black-and-white images do not reveal the color that could be found at Culebra. Machines and men cutting along the sides of the mountain exposed layers and bands of yellow, blue, orange, and earthy red. Green jungle framed the edges of the scene, capped by a bright blue sky, dotted by puffs of white cloud and grayish smoke belching from steam-powered dredges and the darting, coal-burning locomotives. Work on the canal was a combination of color and movement, depth and breadth, men and machines, order and purpose, technology

*This photograph of Contractor's Hill, taken in March 1908, shows the progress men and machines made at Culebra Cut. In the great canyon, a hubbub of rock drills, steam shovels, dirt cars, and dynamite blasts filled the work site.*

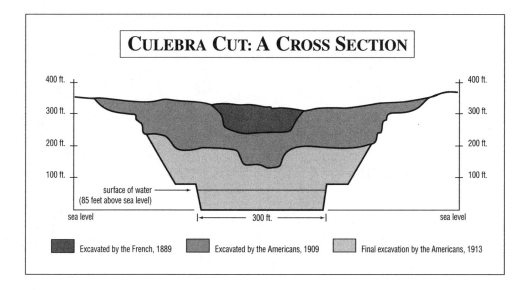

**CULEBRA CUT: A CROSS SECTION**

400 ft. — 400 ft.

300 ft. — 300 ft.

200 ft. — 200 ft.

100 ft. — 100 ft.

surface of water
(85 feet above sea level)

sea level ←——— 300 ft. ———→ sea level

Excavated by the French, 1889   Excavated by the Americans, 1909   Final excavation by the Americans, 1913

and miracles, plus lots of noise. Workers manning hundreds of rock drills sent up a tremendous racket. Adding to the din were the great steam shovels and the trains pushing clattering dirt cars through the cut. Above it all, one could hear the continuous blasts of dynamite. Joseph Bishop, in his book *The Panama Gateway*, published the year the Culebra Cut was completed, described the work along the walls and floor of the cut:

> On either side were the grim, forbidding, perpendicular walls of rock, and in the steadily widening and deepening chasm between—the first man-made canyon in the world—a swarming mass of men and rushing railway trains, monster-like machines, all working with ceaseless activity, all animated seemingly by human intelligence, without confusion or conflict anywhere. . . . The rock walls gave place here and there to ragged sloping banks of rock and earth left by the great slides, covering many acres and reaching far back into the hills, but the ceaseless human activity prevailed everywhere. Everybody knew what he was to do and was doing it, apparently without verbal orders and without getting in the way of anybody else.

Under Goethals's tenure trains hauled thousands of workers in to the cut each morning, just after dawn. Their

*During Goethals's tenure, laborers worked around the clock. The day crews did their best to excavate the canal site, while night crews worked to repair equipment and prepare the work sites for the next day.*

shifts began at 7:00 A.M. sharp and ended at 5:00 P.M. Dynamite crews did their work at midday, while everyone else took a lunch break, as well as during most evenings after 5:00. During the evenings machinery repair crews came into the cut, ready to fix whatever had broken during the day's work. Explosions filled the canyon after dark, as rail crews created new beds for the moveable track lines. The headlamps of the coal trains sent fingers of dancing light through the cut as the train cars deposited their cargo for the steam shovels that would resume their work the next morning.

## THE GREAT DIGGING MACHINES

As work under Goethals progressed, records for cubic yards of earth removed from the cut were made and quickly broken.

Sixty-eight huge steam shovels, the greatest number ever in use at one time, removed over two million cubic yards in March 1909. This figure beat the best month recorded by the French by ten times. One shovel, a ninety-five-ton Bucyrus, set the single shovel record by scooping up seventy thousand cubic yards of earth in less than a month. Each of the gigantic steam shovels at Culebra removed over one million cubic yards before the cut was complete.

These shovels were put to work from one end of the nine-mile cut to the other. But at one place in the cut, near Gold Hill, several of the shovels were in operation, digging at seven different levels, while seven sets of railroad tracks hauled the earth and rock out. During the peak phase of digging at Culebra, 160 trains ran each day, crisscrossing seventy-six miles of canal track, all within the shadow of Culebra Mountain.

*A work crew interrupts its digging to pose for a photograph in front of a steam shovel. Throughout the Canal Zone, these huge mechanical diggers scooped out tons of earth.*

## GIANT DOORS THAT CONSERVE WATER

Each Panamanian canal lock is gigantic. The gates alone, which close off the canal's locks, are a technical marvel. There are forty-six lock gates, their total mass about fifty-eight thousand tons. Each gate has two leaves, or doors, their weight varying from three hundred to six hundred tons. The gates stand between forty-seven and eighty-two feet tall, depending on their place in the locks. Each leaf is sixty-five feet wide and seven feet thick. Attached to the bottom of each leaf is an eighteen-ton sill. Each sill required six million rivets to put it together. When these doors were being constructed, workers could crawl inside through a series of manholes and passages. There they could double-check each rivet. All bad rivets were removed and replaced. Leaks between the gates and the sill on the lock floor are prevented by a rubber seal measuring four inches wide and a half inch thick.

In addition to outer gates each lock, measuring 1,000 feet long, has internal gates spaced at 350 feet and 550 feet. The purpose for these internal doors is to create shorter locks, thus conserving water. Many of the ships that pass through the canal are shorter than one thousand feet long. To conserve millions of gallons of fresh Gatun Lake water, the internal lock gates are used for such ships, because the entire lock does not need to be filled.

Since the gates of each lock are actually just large doors, they must hang on hinges. But most people have never seen hinges like these. The portion of the hinge that fastens to the lock wall weighs between thirty-six thousand and thirty-nine thousand pounds. The part attached to the gate had to be tested and guaranteed to withstand a strain of thirty-five tons before breaking.

*Two laborers stand atop a gigantic unfinished lock gate in this 1913 photograph. The height of a lock gate varies from forty-seven to eighty-two feet, depending on its placement within the lock.*

*A dirt spreader distributes debris at the La Boca dump site, where nearly twenty-two million cubic yards of earth were deposited during the course of the construction.*

During nearly any year of construction, at least one thousand miles of rail lines were in operation up and down the length of the Canal Zone.

Once dirt and stone were excavated from the cut, it had to be hauled away from the work site. Dumping grounds were situated as far as twenty-three miles from Culebra. Much of this debris was simply discarded, used to fill in low, swampy lands, for example. A large part was put to good use, in the building of earthen dams, breakwaters, and bases for new rail lines. All the dumps were closely monitored and maintained, some of them covering up to one thousand acres. Dirt spreaders were used to fan out the debris. The dirt spreader was a railroad car with giant blades on either side. These steel blades, powered by compressed air, pushed newly deposited earth away from the rail line. The largest such dump was at Balboa, formerly La Boca, where twenty-two million cubic yards were deposited, creating nearly seven hundred acres of new Pacific coastland.

*Wrecking cranes attempt to free a mud-caked steam shovel following the Cucaracha Slide. After the slide, debris covered fifty acres and continued to creep farther into the cut.*

All of this work required constant oversight. To ensure that work on the canal could progress rapidly, it was important that each day each man did his job. No part of the excavation— from dynamiting to shoveling, from dirt removal to train movements—could be allowed to interfere with the operation of another part of the process.

## THE CUCARACHA SLIDE

One recurring problem—landslides—often interfered with the project, however. As the work on Culebra Cut pushed deeper and deeper into the earth, the walls of the cut would sometimes collapse. Usually heavy rains occurred before a slide, making the earth muddy and heavy with water. The first slide in the cut occurred on October 4, 1907. Centered on the east bank, south of Gold Hill, the Cucaracha Slide plunged rock and mud into the cut, ripping apart two steam shovels. Since the initial slide took place at night, no one was killed or hurt. Covering an area of about fifty acres, the slide kept moving for days, farther and farther down into the cut. Major Gaillard described it as "a tropical glacier—of mud instead of ice." Over a week later, the slide stopped, and half a million cubic yards of mud lay at the bottom of the cut.

Such slides continued in later years; in 1910 and 1911 serious slides buried everything from steam shovels to locomotives. Track disappeared or was twisted into unusable shapes. Sometimes a slide destroyed weeks of progress on the cut and required months to clean up. All told, at least twenty-two major slides occurred within Culebra and at other canal sites.

The only way engineers and workers could battle slides was to create a cut along the mountainside with an upward angle, called the angle of repose. Workers kept cutting away along the slopes of the cut until the slides stopped.

*To combat landslides in the cut, mountainsides were cut along the angle of repose. Using this method, mountains retained a wider base while gradually becoming narrower toward the peak.*

Such angling might keep the earth from moving downward in such a massive fashion. But such a strategy did not stop the slides completely. In fact, the worst such mishap was the Cucaracha Slide, located just south of Gold Hill on the eastern side of Culebra Cut. The slide was so massive that it slipped across the entire cut and started up the opposite side. This was at least the sixth time a major slide at Cucaracha had destroyed several months' work in short order.

When Goethals and Gaillard went out to survey the damage from this slide, Gaillard was almost speechless. "What are we to do now?" he asked, nearly in shock. Goethals surveyed the wreckage. "Hell," he said matter-of-factly, "dig it out again."

## BUILDING AT GATUN DAM

The work at Culebra Cut was indeed massive in scope, but work elsewhere on the canal was also impressive. To harness

### WOMEN IN THE CANAL ZONE

In the final years of building the Panama Canal, the total workforce added up to between forty-five thousand and fifty thousand. A minority of those in the zone—about six thousand—were white Americans. About twenty-five hundred of those were women and children.

Nearly all the jobs in the Canal Zone, from steam shovel operators to cooks, were done by men. No more than three hundred women were ever employed at one time by the Isthmian Canal Company. A female railroad telegrapher was the best paid among them, receiving $125 a week, compared to the average white male worker's weekly pay of $150.

While bachelors had to share lodgings, married canal workers were given special treatment. Married men who earned less than two hundred dollars a month were provided a furnished, four-room apartment, including bath, and paid no rent. The more money a worker was paid, the better his family's accommodations. An American man earning between three hundred dollars and four hundred dollars was provided a Type 10 house: a two-story model with three bedrooms, living room, dining room, kitchen, and bath, with porches on both levels.

the Chagres River, work began on the Gatun Dam. Compared to the work and hazards of digging in the Culebra Cut, the building of Gatun Dam was easy. The dam consisted of a long, earthen embankment formed from soil and debris removed from various digging sites, especially Culebra Cut, and hauled by rail to the Gatun construction site.

Eventually the dam extended for a mile and a half, harnessing the Chagres River behind this massive wall of earth and rock. The dam was fifteen times as wide across its base as it was across its top to protect it against erosion and washout. The Gatun Locks were built at the eastern end of the dam, and a hydroelectric plant was built along its banks. The dam produced electricity for the canal machinery and for the people of Panama.

Construction on the canal's huge locks began at Gatun in August 1909. Work began a few months later on the canal's

Wives of white American workers could shop in large, department-style stores run by the Isthmian Canal Commission, where everything from pins to sewing machines to baby clothes could be found. Prices in such stores—there were eighteen of them scattered up and down the Canal Zone—were usually lower than back in the United States.

While their husbands worked, women could occupy their time with one of the nine women's clubs in the zone, each located in a different town. Each club boasted a full-time women's club director.

During warm summer evenings couples could take walks, visit a motion picture theater, listen to a band concert, or just sit on the porch, enjoying conversation and the latest news or gossip.

The Isthmian Canal Commission also encouraged black women to come to the Canal Zone in large numbers. Many arrived, ready to go to work as laundresses. Some came to join their husbands or perhaps a brother or father. No housing was provided for black women, however, who were forced to live in shacks and shanties as best they could find shelter. Some basic housing was provided for married black workers, but such dwellings were usually small and crude at best.

*A 1909 photograph reveals the crowded interior of the Gatun Dam hydroelectric plant. The powerful dam produced enough electricity to run the canal machinery and to provide electricity to the people of Panama.*

Pacific side at Pedro Miguel, where ships were to be brought down from Gatun Lake via Miraflores Lake. From there the Miraflores Locks, two of them, dropped passing ships to the Pacific Ocean.

## THE GIANT LOCKS

Each lock dwarfed everything around it. Lock walls stood eighty-one feet high, the height of a five- or six-story building, and measured one thousand feet in length. Standing at the bottom of such a lock, as many visitors to the canal did before these huge concrete reservoirs were filled with water in 1913, people lost their perspective. It was like being surrounded by tall buildings with no doors or windows, nothing to indicate just how big a hole the visitor was standing in.

Other monumental structures in history—the Egyptian pyramids, European castles, river dams, the Washington Monument, for example—had been formed by placing cut stones together. The Panama Canal, however, consisted of huge concrete slabs made from a mixture of sand, gravel, and cement. The Gatun Locks alone required over two million cubic yards of concrete. At Pedro Miguel and Miraflores, over 2.4 million cubic yards were needed.

Each lock was built in thirty-six-foot sections and took about a week to complete. At Gatun cableways, a system of large suspended cables carried great buckets holding six tons of concrete each. Each bucket was swung into position and

*Men standing inside one of the canal's locks are dwarfed by the towering gates in the distance.*

emptied of its contents. The buckets were brought to the site on railway flatcars, two at a time. The empty buckets were returned by flatcar to be filled again.

At Pedro Miguel and Miraflores workers used a series of cranes instead of cableways to deliver their loads. The cranes were moved from place to place on rail tracks. Some of the cranes were built in a T shape, with a bucket suspended on each arm of the T.

The locks, dams, and spillways of the canal required five million sacks and barrels of cement before the job was finished. All of it was shipped from New York State. This concrete was one of the major expenses of building the canal. So much concrete was used that it is estimated that fifty thousand dollars was saved simply by having the cement crews shake the bags out after each was emptied.

### SOMETHING TO CELEBRATE

The work on the Miraflores Locks ended May 17, 1913. The Gatun Locks were completed just two weeks later. But between these dates, another important goal was reached. On May 20 two steam shovels, working from opposite sides of the Culebra Cut, met each other at the bottom level of the mountain basin. Dynamite was exploded, and steam whistles blasted in celebration of the achievement. Men and machines had

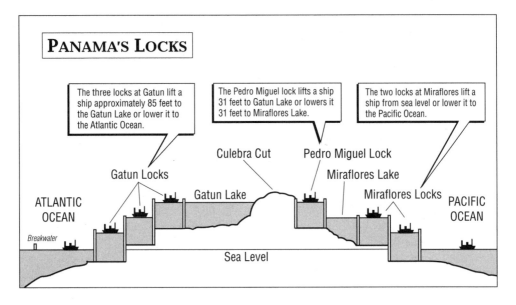

## PANAMA'S LOCKS

The three locks at Gatun lift a ship approximately 85 feet to the Gatun Lake or lower it to the Atlantic Ocean.

The Pedro Miguel lock lifts a ship 31 feet to Gatun Lake or lowers it 31 feet to Miraflores Lake.

The two locks at Miraflores lift a ship from sea level or lower it to the Pacific Ocean.

Culebra Cut    Pedro Miguel Lock

Gatun Locks    Miraflores Lake

ATLANTIC OCEAN    Gatun Lake    Miraflores Locks    PACIFIC OCEAN

Breakwater

Sea Level

*A photograph from 1912 provides a glimpse of Miraflores Locks before the gates were in place. Work on Miraflores was completed on May 17, 1913.*

carved a 370-foot gash in the natural rise. At last the great barrier—Culebra Mountain—had been conquered.

All the canal's major elements were now being completed. The final bucket of concrete was poured at Gatun on May 31, 1913, less than two weeks after the completion of the Culebra Cut. About mid-June the final guard gates at the Gatun Locks were in place. On June 27 the spillway gates were closed at Gatun Dam, allowing the waters of Gatun Lake to begin rising to their full depth.

By September 10, 1913, all dry excavation on the Panama Canal came to an end, as the last load of rock and earth was carried up by the last Bucyrus steam shovel. The last dirt train ran its route out of Culebra. Work crews began removing and destroying whole sections of track. A reporter for the *New York Times* wrote: "The Cut tonight presented an unusual spectacle with hundreds of piles of old ties from the railroad tracks being in flames." All was being readied for the first ship to pass through the canal. Just two weeks later, the first trial of the locks at Gatun was made.

# The Opening
# of the
# Panama Canal

Once the locks were completed at Pedro Miguel in 1911 and Miraflores and Gatun in 1913, the canal was basically finished. The final year, 1913, proved to be the most exciting of all.

Everyone working in the Canal Zone knew that the work was nearly completed. The time was approaching when the first ship could be sent through the new canal. Robert Wood, a U.S. Army officer who had been in the Canal Zone since 1904, wrote:

> Men reported to work early and stayed late, without overtime. . . . I really believe that every American employed would have worked that year without pay, if only to see the first ship pass through the completed Canal. That spirit went down to all the laborers.

On September 26 the time arrived to send a boat through the locks. A small craft was picked, the tugboat *Gatun*, which had

*Building materials clutter this aerial view of the Gatun Locks, photographed in 1913. Only a few months later, the first ship to pass through the Panama Canal would embark on its monumental journey.*

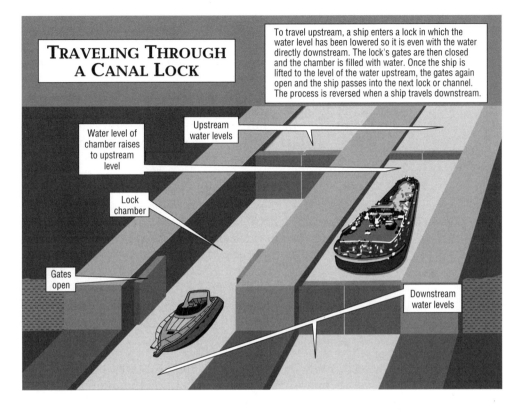

**TRAVELING THROUGH A CANAL LOCK**

To travel upstream, a ship enters a lock in which the water level has been lowered so it is even with the water directly downstream. The lock's gates are then closed and the chamber is filled with water. Once the ship is lifted to the level of the water upstream, the gates again open and the ship passes into the next lock or channel. The process is reversed when a ship travels downstream.

Upstream water levels

Water level of chamber raises to upstream level

Lock chamber

Gates open

Downstream water levels

been used to haul mud barges on the Atlantic side. The tugboat was cleaned up by its crew, who placed flags at both the bow and stern. The *Gatun* was ready to enter the locks at ten o'clock that morning as thousands of people lined the lock walls, gripping the handrails and leaning forward to get a good look.

At a signal from Goethals, the valves were opened, and the waters of Gatun Lake began to fill the lower Gatun Lock. The watching crowds were amused by the sight of hundreds of frogs in the lock, brought fresh from the waters of Gatun Lake. But there was no great rush of water into the lock as many expected. The water poured in slowly, since Gatun Lake was not yet at its full height on that day, and it took much of the afternoon to fill even the lower lock. But by 4:45 the lock was filled, and the small tugboat entered the lower Gatun Lock. In their order, all the locks were filled as the tugboat rose from one to the other.

It was nearly dark when the *Gatun* finished its course through the Gatun Locks. By 6:45 the tugboat was out on the calm waters of Gatun Lake, blowing her whistle to the watching

## LIFE AFTER THE PANAMA CANAL

The story of the building of the Panama Canal includes several important faces and names.

Just as World War I overshadowed the opening of the canal in 1914, so did it come to overshadow the lives of several key figures connected with the building of the canal. Colonel William Gorgas, who spent years fighting yellow fever and malaria, served as head of the U.S. Army medical service during the Great War. He died in England in 1920. Colonel George Goethals was promoted to the rank of major general in 1915. After serving as governor of the Panama Canal Zone until 1916, he was posted during the war in Washington, D.C., as quartermaster general. He continued to work after the war as an independant engineering consultant in New York City. He died of cancer in 1928. His body was buried at the military academy at West Point. Philippe Bunau-Varilla, the Frenchman who worked so hard to ensure the construction on an American canal in Panama, enlisted in the

crowd, which broke into a cheer. The first trial run, called a lockage, was a success. Among the crowd at that moment of triumph was Philippe Bunau-Varilla, watching with tears in his eyes.

Within a couple of weeks President Woodrow Wilson pressed the button in Washington that was attached to telegraph wires leading to Panama and blasted the hole in the dike that let the waters of Gatun Lake into Culebra Cut. Two weeks after that, on October 25, canal dredges and barges were the first to be brought through the Miraflores and Pedro Miguel Locks.

Months passed as some fine tuning on the canal continued. Not until January 7, 1914, did a crane boat, the *Alexandre La Valley*, make the first complete passage through the canal. The boat passed from the Atlantic to the Pacific side. The event received little attention—no fanfare and no ceremony—and almost no one noticed that the first boat to make a complete passage had been abandoned by the French in the Canal Zone years earlier.

### THE ARRIVAL OF THE END

With nearly all the work finished, the process of closing down construction began. Thousands of canal workers, engineers,

French army and fought in the war along the western front. He lost a leg in the Battle of Verdun, and died in 1940 at the age of seventy-nine.

Theodore Roosevelt, whose forceful personality as president guaranteed that the Panama Canal would be an American success, died in January 1919, just five years after the canal was completed. His visit to the Canal Zone in 1906 was his only one to Panama. He never saw the finished canal.

Chief engineer John Stevens, whose organizational skills and knowledge of railroads helped to streamline construction of the canal, did visit Panama in his later years. After leaving the work on the canal in 1907, he continued to work as an engineer in the United States and abroad. In 1917, President Woodrow Wilson sent Stevens to Russia to give assistance in the construction of the Trans-Siberian Railway. Stevens outlived all the other great names connected with the building of the Panama Canal, dying in 1943 at the age of ninety.

steam shovel operators, and laborers were now without jobs and were booking passage for home. The company ordered tool sheds, machine shops, barracks, and engineering offices to be taken apart or simply destroyed. The Isthmian Canal Commission ceased to exist. President Wilson appointed Goethals the first governor of the Panama Canal Zone. There were final parties up and down the Canal Zone, as workers and their families said good-bye to each other. The years of building were over; for many it was time to leave.

## WAR ECLIPSES THE CELEBRATION

Back in the United States Americans were excited by the news of the completed canal. Great celebrations were being prepared in Washington, D.C., and San Francisco. Plans included a flotilla of a hundred warships on the Atlantic coast on New Year's Day of 1915. The ships were to steam south to the canal. Once there, they would pass through and sail in triumph to San Francisco for the opening of a world's fair, the Panama-Pacific International Exposition.

But the epic passage never happened. Just days before August 15, 1914, the date set for the official opening of the

*Onlookers crowd along the sides of the Pedro Miguel Lock while a canal dredge passes through the lock on its way to Culebra Cut.*

Panama Canal, war broke out across Europe. The world's attention focused on Europe, not on the newly opened Panama Canal. With the war on, celebrating seemed pointless. On the fifteenth, the passage of the first official customer for the Panama Canal, a cement boat called the *Cristobal*, was nearly ignored by newspapers. Distracted by war, most Americans for the time being forgot about the completion of a centuries-old dream called the Panama Canal.

# EPILOGUE

With the opening of the canal, one could begin to summarize the numbers involved in its construction. For starters, the total number of cubic yards of earth and rock removed in constructing the canal is 262 million, compared with the French total of 30 million. This is four times the amount Lesseps suggested decades earlier would need to be dug for a *sea-level* canal.

Much of the work had been centered at Culebra Cut, where earth and rock were removed at a cost of ninety million dollars. That represents about ten million dollars a mile at Culebra, which was renamed in 1915 as Gaillard Cut for Colonel David Gaillard, who had directed the work there under Goethals. Gaillard had died of a brain tumor in December 1913. The previous summer he had suffered a mental breakdown, which required him to leave the Canal Zone, never to return. He did not see the tug *Gatun* take the first voyage through the canal.

## THE CANAL'S COST

The cost of the canal must be figured in several ways. In dollars, the total price is staggering. Just figuring what the Americans spent, the bill comes to $352 million. Add in the French expenditures, and the total peaks out at approximately $639 million. In 1914 this made the Panama Canal the greatest single

*When the steam shovels and men finally completed their digging in the canal site, a total of 262 million cubic yards of earth had been excavated.*

construction project in American history. Another cost must be figured, however: the cost in lives. According to American records beginning in 1904, 5,609 workers died from disease and accidents. Add to this the number of French lives, and the number swells to nearly 25,000. That represents about one person for every ten feet across the Canal Zone.

Beyond the numbers, there are other impressive statistics. The canal was completed ahead of schedule by six months, despite delays caused by landslides. The project was finished under budget, as well, by about twenty-three million dollars. The American project was completed, also, without scandal, bribes kickbacks, or corruption. No company was ever accused of having made excessive profits. Much of the credit must go to Goethals, whose honest direction in the zone was nothing short of inspiring.

Traffic during the years of World War I was light, averaging about two thousand ships annually. Within ten years of opening about five thousand ships were taken through the canal each year. Since 1960 the canal has handled from twelve thousand to fifteen thousand ships annually. As many as fifty ships transit the canal daily, and it handles traffic twenty-four hours a day. The length of the average transit is about eight hours.

Tolls were set originally at ninety cents a cargo ton in 1914, and they were not raised until 1974, when the rate increased to $1.08. Today, tolls are set according to the value of a ship's

*The Pedro Miguel Lock as it appeared on June 13, 1910. The Americans spent an incredible $352 million to build the Panama Canal. This enormous figure was $23 million under its original budget.*

*Twelve thousand to fifteen thousand ships pass through the Panama Canal annually. The standard transit through the canal takes eight hours and costs an average of sixteen thousand dollars per ship.*

cargo. The average toll per ship is approximately sixteen thousand dollars. By law the canal must pay for itself and charge enough to at least break even.

In 1979 two new Panama Canal treaties went into effect. Under these treaties, the United States–administered Canal Zone ceased to exist, with Panama taking back its territory. The United States has also agreed to give up operating control of the canal by December 31, 1999. The United States will still guarantee the neutrality of the canal and retains the right to defend it against hostile nations.

Over eight decades have passed since the opening of the Panama Canal. In 1914 this great achievement represented the end of tremendous planning and hard work. Many lives were lost; yet the work on the canal continued until this monumental task was finished. Today the Panama Canal remains as vital and significant as ever. The canal still serves as the most important link between the Atlantic and Pacific, symbolizing the benefits of cooperation between the many nations of the world.

# For Further Reading

Bob Considine, *The Panama Canal*. New York: Random House, 1951.

Lerner Publications, Department of Geography staff, *Panama in Pictures*. Minneapolis: Lerner Publications, 1987.

Shirlee Newman and Diane Sherman, *Canals*. Chicago: Melmont Publishers, 1964.

*Panama*. Let's Visit Places and Peoples of the World Series. New York: Chelsea House, 1988.

R. Conrad Stein, *The Story of the Panama Canal*. Cornerstones of Freedom Series. Chicago: Childrens Press, 1982.

Judith St. George. *The Panama Canal: Gateway to the World*. New York: Putnam Publishing Group, 1989.

# Works Consulted

Charles Beatty, *De Lesseps of Suez: The Man and His Times*. New York: Harper and Brothers, 1956.

I. Bennett, *History of the Panama Canal*. New York: Gordon Press, 1976.

Joseph Bucklin Bishop, *The Panama Gateway*. New York: Charles Scribner's Sons, 1913.

Kevin Buckley, *Panama: The Whole Story*. New York: Simon and Schuster, 1991.

Miles P. Du Val, *And the Mountains Will Move: The Story of the Building of the Panama Canal*. 1947. Reprint, Westport, CT: Greenwood, 1969.

Frederic J. Haskin, *The Panama Canal*. New York: Doubleday, Page and Company, 1913.

Walter LaFeber, *The Panama Canal: The Crisis in Historical Perspective*. New York: Oxford University Press, 1978.

John Marlowe, *World Ditch*. New York: Macmillan, 1964.

David McCullough, "A Man, a Plan, a Canal, Panama!" *American Heritage*, June 1971.

———, *The Path Between the Seas: The Creation of the Panama Canal, 1870–1914*. New York: Simon and Schuster, 1977.

W. Leon Pepperman, *Who Built the Panama Canal?* New York: E. P. Dutton, 1915.

John Frank Stevens, *An Engineer's Recollections*. New York: McGraw-Hill, 1936.